The Science of Numerology

The Science of Numerology

Discerning What Numbers Mean to You

WALTER B. GIBSON

A Newcastle Classic

Originally published in 1927 by George Sully & Company of New York.

ISBN: 0-87877-230-8
A Newcastle Classic
First printing 1995
10 9 8 7 6 5 4 3 2 1
Printed in the United States of America.

PREFACE

The purpose of this book is to give a modern view-point on an ancient subject, in a way that will prove interesting and helpful to the reader.

It does not seek to establish a new system of philosophy, or to over-emphasize the importance of long-stored knowledge. Instead, it endeavors to acquaint the reader with information that is well worth knowing.

The subject of Numerology does not become technical and involved as one goes further into its study. Instead, each step leads toward a definite objective; the scientific interpretation of numbers and their significance in the affairs of daily life.

Since the beginning of the recent revival of interest in Numerology, there has been great need for a book on the subject that would give more than a hasty, sketchy outline of the principles of the science; yet which would not burden and confuse the reader with abstruse calculations. This volume is a sincere effort to supply that need.

The book contains twenty-two chapters, symbolic of the twenty-two primary and secondary numbers of Numerology.

The early chapters deal with the significance of numbers, and the later chapters explain the importance of those numbers to people.

He who seeks for strange and remarkable coincidences, based upon the sequences and interpretations of numbers, will find them in Chapter XX.

TABLE OF CONTENTS

vii

THE KEY TO NUMEROLOGY

The whole science of Numerology depends upon this simple key. Use it for reference as you read the book.

There are nine primary numbers which have vibratory influences. They are 1, 2, 3, 4, 5, 6, 7, 8, 9.

Every number may be reduced to one of those numbers by simply adding its figures; thus 53 equals 8 (5 plus 3), 69 equals 15 and 15 equals 6.

To find the vibratory number of a date take the figures in the month, the day and the year. The third of March 1906 contains the figures 3 (for March), 3 (for the Third) and 1, 9, 0, 6. These figures total 22, which reduces to the vibratory number 4.

The letters of the alphabet each have a special value, thus:

A—1	F—8	K—2	P—8	U—6
B—2	G—3	L—3	Q—1	V—6
C—2	H—8	M—4	R—2	W—6
D—4	I—1	N—5	S—3	X—6
E—5	J—1	O—7	T—4	Y—1
	Z—7	TH—9	PH—8	

To find the vibratory number of a name add the values of the letters and reduce; thus John Doe totals 37 = 10 = 1.

THE VIBRATORY NUMBERS that are of importance to you are (1) The Number of the Date of your Birth. (2) The Number to which the letters of your full name reduce. (3) The Number of the name you commonly use.

THE SCIENCE OF
NUMEROLOGY

I. INTRODUCTION

THE SCIENCE AND HISTORY OF
NUMEROLOGY

The science of Numerology is the practical application of the fundamental laws of mathematics to the material existence of man.

There is no occult or supernatural power in numbers themselves. They serve as the key to the natural sequence of events, and have always been of great utility to mankind. They form a universal language, requiring no interpreter in so far as their primary uses are concerned.

But every language is more than mere words. It serves as a medium for the expression of ideas. In the same way, numbers, the symbols of the earliest language, carry meanings and express themselves.

The discovery of the significance of numbers requires study. The computations of higher mathematics exist, even though millions of people

1

do not know how to use them. So do the meanings of numbers exist; but they must be studied before they become thoroughly understood.

Numerology explains and reveals many facts; but always through a natural means. If a man states that a certain day seventy years from now will fall on Monday, we realize that he has made a true prediction of a future event; but we do not call him a fortune teller. We know that he is a mathematician, and we see nothing strange or supernatural in the calculations of an astronomer who tells us when a certain comet will appear. A thousand years ago, such a man would have been called a necromancer—a master of the Black Art. In these enlightened times he is hailed as a scientist.

So when a Numerologist, by a system of computation based upon the interpretations of numbers, states that the vibratory influences of a certain period are indicative of specific results, he is not hazarding a chance guess, but he is working out a peculiar problem that depends upon interpretation rather than calculation.

Interpretations do not possess the reliability of exact calculations. It is difficult to transpose thoughts, with all their shades of meaning, from one language to another; and it is a greater task to express the ideas of numbers in the artificial form of words. Yet the general meaning, even though imperfectly expressed, can usually be obtained through a knowledge of Numerology.

Numbers, although they may become highly complicated, are really very simple. The nine figures and the cipher form the basis for long mathematical problems. Similarly, Numerology depends entirely upon the figures, or primary numbers, and its elementary principles may be easily learned.

The chapters that follow explain the significance of numbers, and each chapter deals with its particular phase of Numerology, so that the subject becomes quite clear as the reader progresses step by step.

The history of Numerology dates from prehistoric times.

The earliest civilization we know of gave significance to certain numbers. The ancient Egyptians developed numbers to a high degree, and, at a later date, the science of numbers reached its highest stage of interpretation in its relation to the Hebrew alphabet.

The modern trend has been to develop mathematics, and to establish a more practical alphabet, with the aim of increasing the efficiency of language. This has resulted in a gradual decline in the interpretation of the meanings of numbers through the medium of letters and words.

A Renaissance is now occurring. New interest

has been revived in the ancient science of Numerology; and although many important discoveries have been lost, it is probable that the new Numerology will prove of great value in the development of modern civilization; for the demands of today call for practical knowledge rather than pedantic learning of the type which flourished in Mediæval times.

II. THE PRIMARY NUMBERS AND
THEIR POWERS

There are nine primary numbers in Numerology.

They are represented by the figures 1, 2, 3, 4, 5, 6, 7, 8, and 9. All the higher numbers embody certain characteristics of those numbers; and all the higher numbers may be reduced to a primary number.

Thus the number 53, which is composed of 5 and 3, reduces to the primary number 8, the sum of 5 and 3. The number 67, composed of 6 and 7, reduces to 13, the sum of 6 and 7; and 13, in turn, being composed of 1 and 3, reduces to 4.

Each of the primary numbers possesses what is called a "vibratory influence." Through this, it gives certain indications of normal characteristics of the individual who possesses that vibratory number.

Now there are very nice distinctions between the tendencies of the different numbers. Some possess qualities held by others; some have qualities which are distinctively their own, yet which seem to be similar to those of other numbers.

The only way in which the vibratory influence

of each primary number may be properly understood is through the complete consideration of each separate and independent number. That will be taken up in the following pages, and will be followed by a summary of the conflicts and harmonies of the various numbers. The reader should study carefully the particular numbers which are of importance to himself, as will be explained in the chapters dealing with the determination of numbers. As a basis of consideration, the following outline is given for preliminary consideration.

There are nine types of man, as indicated by the primary numbers of Numerology. They may be summarized as follows:

1. The Aggressive, or Courageous Type. It produces explorers, pioneers, generals, and rulers.

2. The Placid, or Balanced Type. It produces physicians, nurses, professors, diplomats, and home-lovers.

3. The Expressive, or Active Type. It produces actors, orators, singers, authors, musicians, artists, dancers, and signifies the artistic temperament.

4. The Deliberate, or Cautious Type. It produces steady workers, secretaries, accountants, mechanics, and chemists.

5. The Versatile or Restless Type. It produces travelers, globe-trotters, adventurers, and

promotors; and it also develops the artistic temperament, but not to the degree of number 3.

6. The Dependable, or Considerate Type. It produces home-lovers, constant workers, scientists, and also authors and actors of a high type. It has artistic qualities, and develops philosophers, teachers, and brilliant preachers.

7. The Mystic, or Melancholy Type. It produces deep thinkers, propounders of new theories, dreamers, poets, vivid authors and dramatists, and persons who sometimes rise to sudden fame. It is the indication of Stoicism, and brings leaders in new movements and religions.

8. The Successful, or Powerful Type. It produces lawyers, statesmen, leaders, conquerors, successful business men and millionaires.

9. The Universal, or Magnetic Type. It produces great scientists and brilliant artists; philanthropists, actors, singers and musicians. It also develops visionaries and idealists.

The numbers 10, 11, and 22 have sometimes been included with the primary numbers of Numerology. They are, however, secondary numbers and will be discussed in a later chapter. The erroneous conception of these numbers has been brought about through the fact that all the numbers from 1 to 22 have certain minor qualities, as each one represents a letter in the Hebrew alphabet, upon which the Kabbala of numbers is based.

Number 10 is often thought of as a primary number, but it is not; for it is simply a form of the number 1. In the same way, numbers 11 and 22 are mentioned because, being the lowest and highest of the secondary numbers, they have more marked tendencies than the others. But they are irregular and of minor consequence and have nothing in common with the primary numbers.

The number 0 is not considered in Numerology, for it is not representative of a quantity. We use it in notation merely as a form of convenience. It has no vibratory influence in human affairs, for while it means a lack of quantity, it is also the symbol of universality. It is paradoxical in nature, and being something, yet nothing, it comes beyond the sphere of human existence, and has no interpretation that may be considered tangible. It is an attempt to represent the infinite, and its very form, the circle, is symbolic of that attempt; for the circle has no beginning and no ending, and is the nearest mortal conception to the boundlessness of time and space. The cipher is infinite, yet infinitesimal.

It should be remembered that figures are merely the means employed to express definite quantities. Every number has a power, not expressed by the figure; and that power denotes quality. The qualities of those numbers are expressed through Numerology.

So the following pages should be studied with that thought in mind; with the knowledge that each number is something more than a mere representation of straight and curved lines.

The quality of a number is the thought upon which it is based; and the vibratory influence of the number is the expression of that thought.

It should be noted throughout that there is no Type of Genius among the nine primary numbers, and their vibrations. This is because genius is a strange, unaccountable development that cannot be definitely ascribed to any primary number, yet which may appear unexpectedly and in an unexplainable manner in any number.

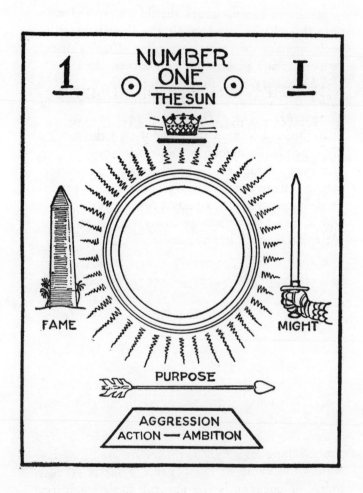

III. THE VIBRATION OF NUMBER 1

Number 1 is the symbol of Unity.

It is a simple, yet powerful number, representing definiteness of purpose; but at the same time it is limited, and is generally restricted to a single, definite field.

It indicates unswerving action, a desire for achievement which cannot be turned from its goal, nor be disturbed in its progress. Being the foundation of all other numbers, it is stalwart, self-centered, and powerful; yet restricted.

Number 1 is significant of the highest point; for in all the affairs of mankind *one* person or thing is always regarded as the greatest, strongest or finest. Number 1 is the unit of life; the concept of the individual, and the fundamental beginning of all things. It is the Alpha, or the beginning, and it stands for power of self, isolation and independence.

It is a significant fact that a child's mind grasps the meaning of other numbers before it understands the value of number 1. That is because unity, or oneness, is the natural, basic condition. If there is just one specimen, or thing of a particular type, the existence of that particular thing is a fact. Thus the number 1 stands for existence, and its expression as a number is merely a matter of convenience, made necessary because of the use of other numbers.

The number 1 stands for centralization, because when a subject is studied or discussed, one type or one example is taken as the basis for study. We speak of the human mind, the automobile, the ocean, or the sea-shore, and in that way bring our thoughts to a centralized point of unity. It is only by concentrated study of a single subject that a person may utilize the full force of his mentality. The individual person must look upon the world from his own view-point; if he tries to see it through the eyes of other people, his impressions will be imperfect and artificial, and will never be really clear until they have been translated to his own view-point.

As an illustration of the unity of the human mind, try to visualize two separate scenes at one time. A clear mental picture will be impossible; the mind will shift from one scene to the other, and will not record simultaneous impressions. The ultimate result will be a centralization on one scene, and a gradual elimination of the other.

Thus number 1 is seen to be the number of concentration, application, and effort.

Number 1 is symbolized by the Sun, the center

of the solar system, and the greatest body of our material realm.

The person who comes under the vibratory influence of number 1 will be characterized by definiteness of purpose and a love of constant progress. He will not strive for any great goal unless his present path leads directly to it, so that he can visualize the full course ahead. He will not be dismayed by obstacles, and will generally overcome them; and he will meet issues squarely, with no attempt to avoid them.

Thus we find that the good characteristics of number 1 are self-reliance, produced by belief of ability; distinction, gained by forcefulness, and power of achievement; dignity, the outgrowth of self-interest and desire for advancement; leadership, gained as a result of progressive activity; inventive genius, due to the ability of concentration and singleness of interest; and, above all, power and definiteness of purpose.

On the contrary, number 1 has its faults as a vibratory number. Theoretically, progress along a specific line is good; but practically it often produces a one-track mind, incapable of absorbing advice, foolishly insistent despite overwhelming odds, and incapable of giving up an object unworthy of attainment.

The principal fault of the vibratory influence of number 1 is selfishness, which is caused by centralization of purpose. Domination is also a shortcoming, for the person who finds that it gains certain advantages will often resort to it. Lack of forethought and the inability to heed the advice of other people often mar the careers of people of this type; and they frequently suffer because of their lack of coöperation. Narrow-mindedness is a great drawback to an individual controlled by number 1; for such people find it hard to give due credit to the fields in which other people are striving; they cannot see any other goal in life except the one that corresponds with their own ambitions.

It will generally be noticed that when a person who has the vibratory influence of number 1 finds a field of endeavor which is suitable to him, he will never change it. People of this type who have been successful can trace a straight course back to the beginning of their advancement; a course which has had the one definite goal in mind all along.

It should not be supposed that the number 1 type of individuality is utterly incapable of change, or modification; human nature is too adaptable for that. But while this vibration may show certain flexibility, the great trait of the individual is to measure all affairs of life by one's own. A person of this type may definitely decide that fame is the great goal of life; and having so decided, he will see no reason why any other person should have ambitions which do not set fame as the greatest of all purposes. Similarly, the desire for material wealth may become the object of the individual; and in seeking or attaining wealth, the person influenced by number 1 will consider any other purpose in life as foolish, or of little consequence.

Persons influenced by number 1 are by no means unimaginative; but they like to have dreams that may be realized, and they will persistently strive to attain something that other people would give up as hopeless. They are often very friendly, and thoughtful of others, because they realize that to be so will prove advantageous. This is a very fine attribute, because, even though it may be attributed to personal desire, the person who has found it successful will make it a constant practice throughout life, and will gain a helpful, likable personality. Those who are influenced by number 1, but who neglect this phase of development will injure their own interests, and will never know why; they will become more and more self-centered, and may fall under influences that will gradually turn their powerful efforts into wasteful channels.

What number 1 requires is broadness of ideas and constant thought of the future. Friendliness, human interest, and consideration of others are qualities that should be cultivated. This vibratory influence indicates a character which cannot be ruled or suppressed, yet which may be modified and directed into fields of usefulness. It is like the power of a mighty river, which cannot be thwarted in its purpose to reach the sea. Just as some rivers are violent, raging torrents that sweep aside everything in their path, so are some persons uncontrollable and thoughtless in their desire to reach the goal. On the contrary, the well-developed nature of number 1 is like a smoothly running river; great and powerful, yet pleasant, calm, and useful.

Number 1 indicates an indomitable spirit, a thirst for adventure and knowledge as a means of achievement, and an unswerving progress toward a desired or established goal.

People who possess 1 as a vibratory number are loved and admired by many; but they are also liable to form enemies among those whom they sweep aside in their desire for progress.

Culture, education and refinement are of great value—in fact are almost essential—in the development of anyone who has the vibratory number of 1. Such influences are broadening, and they invariably bring out the good qualities of the individual.

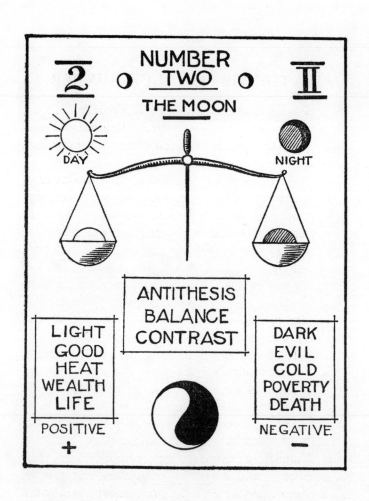

IV. THE VIBRATION OF NUMBER 2

Number 2 is the symbol of Diplomacy.

It is an even number, representing balance and equilibrium; yet at the same time constant fluctuation and changing.

It is the number of antithesis; it indicates a dual nature. It is the number of opposites, significant both of conjunction and separation. It represents day and night, positive and negative, heat and cold, wealth and poverty, good and evil, friendship and enmity, life and death. Thus it forms a completed nature of material conception.

Contrast is fundamental. One of the earliest lessons in life is the acquired knowledge of distinguishing two things; of forming a primitive classification. Likes and dislikes are distinctive. Experience quickly teaches us the things that are desirable and the things that are not. The number 2 stands for symmetry, and when a unit is incomplete in itself, it is generally made perfect through the addition of its counterpart.

Number 2 carries more complications than number 1; and it satisfies conditions that number 1 cannot. As soon as the progressive equilibrium of number 1 has been lost, the balance and certainty of number 2 is required.

Number 2 stands for justice; the equitable settlement between two conflicting interests, each of which is firm in its own belief. With justice come harmony and gentleness; yet, at the same time, the number 2 tells of conflicting ideas that can never be reconciled. The north pole and the south pole are similar; yet they are diametrically opposite. Land and sea are opposed to each other; but they are typified by number 2.

The desirability of any thing is determined by its opposite. People long for wealth because it eliminates poverty; for fame, because it does away with obscurity.

Caution is instinctive in many natures; and it finds its highest development in the vibratory influence of number 2. There is nothing headlong about this number; it typifies carefulness and deliberation.

Number 2 is symbolized by the Moon, which is ever-changing, yet complete and regular, possessing a gentle, yet noticeable influence.

Gentleness of nature is an important characteristic of those who come under the vibratory influence of number 2. It shows a desire for fairness, a sacrifice of self, and thoughtful consideration. The person who has this influence will often be unselfish to a fault.

Another good quality is that of tactfulness.
People of this number are invariably diplomatic
and they always try to create harmony between
conflicting interests.   They are natural peace-
makers.

The home-loving instinct is also found to a
great degree in the vibratory influence of number
2. This is accentuated by the natural desire for
peace and happiness. The creation of harmonious conditions that can be easily balanced is very
suitable and pleasing to the person influenced by
number 2.

These people may never achieve fame; and
they may never be considered as wielders of power; but their real importance will often be great,
though under-rated. Their great desire being
to promote harmony, they will often suggest
courses of action to more aggressive people, who
will take advantage of the suggestions and carry
them through to a successful conclusion.

Many great achievements, many reconciliations,
and many successful partnerships have been
brought about through the unselfish efforts of
persons having the vibratory influence of number
2, who have been content in the belief that "Vir-
tue is its own reward," and who have, therefore,
taken a silent part in events where glory might be
gained.

A highly developed number 2 nature will not

pass unrecognized. The good attributes of this vibration are well understood and appreciated; but the inherent desire of number 2 is that of quietness and normalcy. A nature of this type does not become depressed anod melancholy because others gain temporary fame. The true desires of number 2 are more easily gained and fulfilled.

The social instinct is also present in the vibratory influence of number 2. Two persons of entirely different types, who have conflicting influences and who can never understand each other will often have a common friend in some person of number 2 vibration. In fact, it is the social instinct that often enables a person of this type to attain happiness and to quietly achieve his moderate ambitions. People influenced by the vibration of number 2 are sympathetic, and can easily imagine themselves in other people's places. They understand human nature and makes the best of friends.

Their imaginative dispositions, however, while often to their advantage, are sometimes very harmful to their own interests. As these people are easily satisfied, they are quite adaptive, and sometimes they are too easily contented with conditions that present only a temporary harmony.

They are very changeable. They enjoy contrast as well as harmony, and they will often go to great extremes, looking forward to one thing today, and desiring something else tomorrow.

As they are fond of social life, they will frequently sacrifice permanent interests for the temporary happiness found in agreeable surroundings and good fellowship. They dislike arguing, and will often go far out of their way and put themselves to great inconvenience in order to avoid some trivial issue.

This also brings about a tendency toward procrastination. Anything which is undesirable to the number 2 temperament is instinctively avoided. People influenced by this vibration will promise themselves that they will attend to some matter in the near future, and the near future will always be tomorrow. They themselves feel distressed at their own inability to carry things through, and when they are criticized for their delay, they will plead guilty to the charge, but will rarely change their course of action.

Over-passiveness is another fault commonly found under this vibration. Content with existing comforts seems to be an ever-present quality. Thoughts of a difficult future may arouse a temporary desire for action; but the usual result is a lapse into old ways, and a secret thought that the future will take care of itself.

Aggressiveness is something that a person of this vibration should seek to gain, even though it may be distasteful. An individual influenced by number 2 will never become domineering and self-centered, so he or she should never fear to take action when the time demands it.

Strength of purpose can never injure the number 2 nature. If it is attained, it will bring about a high development of the fine underlying qualities.

Number 2 is too placid. It indicates a willingness to put up with mediocre conditions, and to make too many sacrifices. It is a number that presents great possibilities for development; yet indicates that those possibilities may be wasted because of failure to advance them.

V. THE VIBRATION OF NUMBER 3

Number 3 is the symbol of Versatility.

It is a number that stands for ultimate completeness, reaching beyond the temporary fulfillment of number 2.

It stands for the active agencies of time: the past, the present and the future. It represents the family and desire for broad achievement.

It is the sign of the triangle, and indicates the three dimensions. It embodies powers of both 1 and 2, representing a greater force than either of them.

The number 3 has always had a great significance in the affairs of mankind. It has a somewhat mystical meaning, and there is a tendency naturally to divide activities into three parts, as King Alfred separated the day into three eight-hour periods: one for work; the second for leisure; and the third for sleep.

Just as the triangle is uneven, yet harmonious, so is number 3. It is symbolized by the planet Mars, powerful, strong, and fearless.

The first great characteristic found under number 3 is that of independence. There is a sense of achievement and strength in the number that means security and freedom. Independence is the keynote of the number, for it is the underlying influence of the other attributes of number 3.

Fearlessness follows independence. If the nature of the vibratory influence of 3 is well developed, it will stimulate courage, and will clear the way toward great achievement.

From number 2, the number 3 gains two important things, just as it shows the active power of number 1. One of these attributes is diplomacy; the other is adaptability. Despite its constant activity, the number 3 nature will quickly sense the time for tact, something which is not instinctive in number 1. Yet number 3 does not depend upon tactfulness as does number 2. The quality is ever-present, but only makes itself known when really needed. A person influenced by number 3 will quickly change a subject and carry it into a new channel when occasion demands. It is exuberance, not quietness, that is the most powerful aid in this direction.

The adaptability of number 3 also finds a different outlet than that of number 2. Number 3 does not simply harmonize itself with new conditions; it produces and finds new fields for itself, and the result is versatility. It seems as though an active person influenced by this number can succeed in almost any endeavor, and can do one thing as well as another.

As a result, number 3 is often indicative of talent. It produces people who have real ability that is not restricted to any one course of action.

Few people with this vibration worry about making their way through life. They have a natural capability for taking care of themselves, and finding work that is agreeable. They often enjoy great success, but as a rule they make quick and temporary progress; for they take past experiences, apply them actively to the present, and thus create new fields for the future. They prefer to develop the greatest present opportunity rather than to build slowly toward some future and distant goal. They do not care to wait for the knock of Opportunity; instead they go forth in search of Opportunity itself.

With all these natural qualifications, it is only logical that number 3 should not be disturbed by worry. Gaiety and enthusiasm are two of the most noteworthy qualities of this vibration. Having found a new field of endeavor, a person influenced by this number leaps into the new work with an active pleasure, and drives ahead with a care-free disposition that cannot fail to achieve results. The enthusiasm of 3 is contagious, and it often sweeps aside obstacles and clears the path for progress. Even the most conservative

natures are affected by it.   Number 3 is a "go-
getter."

The happiness and exuberance of this number
enable people influenced by it to laugh at failure,
and to immediately devise some new plan of action that will produce the desired result.   It is a
sweeping force of attainment, and some of the
happiest people in this world have the vibration
of number 3.

People who have this vibration are often uni-
versally admired, and have many friends.   They
love popularity, and that often becomes a fault;
for they may sacrifice real attainments to take up
activities that will be more pleasing to their care-
free spirits.

In them is found the fault of indifference.
They care not for the criticism of the world at
large if they feel that they are on the way to an
attainment that will vindicate them.   They think
more of popularity than they do of esteem.

Furthermore, their gaiety and exuberance are
sometimes so active and outstanding that they
lose all seriousness of disposition.   True, they
will always be tactful, but in a trivial way; and
they will, as a result, disappoint many persons who
are more serious-minded.

The sweeping activity of those under the vibratory influence of number 3 is often very misleading.   People who witness some of their quick

achievements begin to expect great things of them, and then become disappointed to see them suddenly drop what they are doing to go into something else. The number 3 nature is often misunderstood by those who are conservative; and the good beginnings of number 3 are not always lasting.

In the same way, the spirit of number 3 which does not regard work as a difficult or serious undertaking often leads to extravagance. The old saying "Easy come, easy go" is typified by number 3. When a peron of this vibration rises to sudden fame or popularity, he feels confident that he can easily repeat his success, and so he loses no time in gratifying any extravagant desires.

It is true that number 3 thinks of the future, as well as the past. But therein lies the great fault. A person of this nature who has been successful in several ways considers the past, present and future as one. He does not carry the illusion that the future will take care of itself; but he believes that he can take care of the future, and he points to the past and the present as proof of his capability.

During the periods between achievements, a person influenced by number 3 will become careless, and will have no worries, always believing that a "come-back" is only a matter of time. Thus we sometimes see people of this type who are past middle age, and unsettled, who are quite confident that they will soon achieve something worthwhile, and who still have the hopefulness of youth, forgetful that they no longer possess their former strength and endurance.

The qualities most needed by number 3 are centralization of effort; a real purpose to keep at one thing, and carry it through, building it up for future use. They should feel that when they have gained some success, their real interest lies in constantly striving along the same line, even though a slack period may set in. They should not toss real opportunity aside, merely because something else presents more immediate attraction.

They should also seek to cultivate effort. Their ease of accomplishment is often due to the fact that they have natural aptitude. If their talent and versatility are coupled with a willingness of constant effort, the result will be a powerful combination toward achievement.

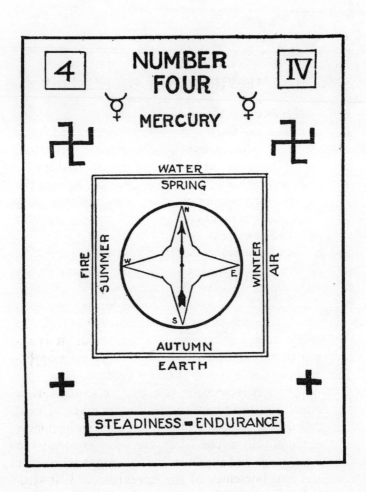

VI. THE VIBRATION OF NUMBER 4

Number 4 is the symbol of Solidity.

It is a stalwart number but is restricted in its scope, and stands for a definite sphere of action, with little departure from established position.

It is a number of the commonplace, lacking the brilliant or singular characteristics of other numbers. It is a number of useful purpose, constant toil, and monotony.

Number 4 is significant of passive strength. It stands for the square, equally and symmetrically divided, yet lacking the unique qualities of other numbers. It is a number of foundation, of steadiness, and things that endure; yet like all the things that we commonly see about us, it is accepted as a matter of course, and is little appreciated.

It is represented by such figures as the Greek cross, and the swastika. It is a number of definite establishment, and its steadiness and firmness is seen in the effects of nature. It represents the four winds and the four directions. It stands for the four horsemen of the Apocalypse. It is symbolized by the four walls of a building. And, like all the commonplace things of life, it is necessary and much needed, yet is not immune from destruction and misfortune. It is a number which is good in its very nature yet which is binding and prevents great achievement. It stands for the toiling of humanity.

Number 4 is symbolized by the planet Mercury, sometimes favorable, sometimes unfavorable, always influenced by the power of stronger and more certain agencies.

There are good characteristics of the number 4; in fact, all the bad qualities are really caused by lack of outstanding good ones.

Regularity and deliberation are noteworthy of number 4. People who have this vibratory influence will fit themselves into regular lines of work, and will go on through life without yearning for things that are beyond their means of attainment.

Strength of purpose is another good point. While high ambition is not found under 4, usefulness predominates; and were it not for the nature of people who have this number, many disagreeable jobs would never be done. Regular duties, that offer little reward, are properly performed and burdensome tasks are constantly executed by the people of this number.

Steadfastness goes with strength of purpose; and endurance naturally follows steadfastness.

Many unsung heroes who have slowly but surely progressed in the face of gigantic obstacles have raised a silent tribute to the vibration of 4.

People who have this vibration are frequently content to use all their effort to achieve small results. They build for the future, and are painstaking: but at the same time they often fail to grasp opportunities, and are opposed to undertaking progressive enterprises that require effort in unrecognized fields.

There are, therefore, many shortcomings in the number. Slowness is sometimes a great fault. Imagination is generally lacking, except as applied to small and established things. Broadness of vision is a needed quality under this vibration.

With the lack of inspiration found in number 4, there is also a tendency toward over-exactness. This sometimes proves to be of great value, but at the same time it often restricts the individual and makes him apply really great and powerful effort to affairs that are hardly worthy of much attention.

There is a crudeness and a clumsiness also present in number 4. The plodding nature will not often seek to develop itself and try to better existing methods. It is content to go its way along channels that have been drained of real achievement.

There is a certain ability for scientific achievement that is found in number 4. What it lacks in brilliancy, it often makes up for in steady effort. There is always the possibility that a person of this vibration may develop something of great consequence by sticking at a task which has become distasteful to other persons.

Number 4 has sometimes been called the symbol of defeat, poverty, and misery. This is hardly a fair estimate of the qualities of the number, and it has probably been brought about through a lack of understanding of the real virtues of the number. It is true that many persons with the vibratory influence of 4 have failed to gain recognition or achievement, and have sunk into misery; but their unfortunate state can be attributed either to inability to cope with unexpected situations, or to a misguided departure from their true field of endeavor.

The number 4 can be highly developed; but it is a great mistake for a person of this vibration to try to cast aside all conventionalities and traditions. They should seek to apply their efforts to tasks that will bring fair return, where they will find appreciation, and can work to good advantage with persons of more active vibrations.

Education is of great importance to the person of number 4; but the education should be practical in nature, enabling the individual to attain a position where he can always be useful, and find his services needed.

Too many persons of the vibration of 4 have let themselves fit into ruts where skill and knowledge are not essential. Then, finding themselves unemployed, they have neither the brilliancy to gain a new opening, nor the capability to demand recognition in the field wherein they were formerly situated.

The great lesson to be learned is that of self-development. The majority of people having the vibration of 4 usually find that their true happiness lies in a field of regular endeavor. They are like the supporting stones of a building; and there is a place for every one. But the individual has some choice in the matter; he can develop himself so that he will be valuable in a position of importance and security. So these people should always strive for higher and better things, with the realization that although progress may be slow, attainment is within their power.

VII. THE VIBRATION OF NUMBER 5

Number 5 is the symbol of Uncertainty.

It is the great number of expansion; yet it is unequal in nature, many-sided and difficult to analyze. It is a shifting, changing, restless number that carries no constant vibration, and that often produces the unexpected.

It indicates vivacity, but also instability. It is filled with uncontrolled activity, and carries quick and sudden changes. It may fall from the heights of achievement to the depths of despair; or it may rise, phœnix-like, from the ashes of defeat to a new glory and triumphant success.

Number 5 is represented by the pentagon, the five-sided figure; regular, but unequal; symmetrical, but unbalanced.

It is also the sign of the star; and like a star in the heavens it shines with great brilliancy, casting its power in boundless directions. Just as a bright star, proud in its brilliancy, fades into oblivion with the coming of day, only to regain its place at night, so does number 5 have its periods of power and its periods of obscurity.

Number 5 is indefinable. Its characteristics

can never be thoroughly determined. It is not dependable and disappointing at times when expectations have been aroused; yet it is also equal to emergencies that require prompt and heroic action. Its vibratory influence may be very good, or very bad; and the only thing consistent about the number is its inconsistency.

Nevertheless, this paradoxical number carries certain characteristics that are easy to recognize, because they are just the things that can be expected of it.

Number 5 is symbolized by Jupiter, the greatest of the planets, yet not always the brightest; a real power and a high influence toward good results.

The person who comes under the influence of 5 will possess a great versatility, but not of the type found in number 3. He will be more of a jack-of-all trades than a man of many achievements, and his natural aptitude in many directions will often retard progress rather than lead to achievement.

Dexterity and cleverness are noteworthy attributes. These qualities can be raised to a high degree of usefulness; in fact they are natural and instinctive. The person influenced by number 5 can always do the right thing at the right time, if he or she will follow natural inclinations. But, unfortunately, there are contradictory influences that often prove injurious.

Number 5 is filled with enthusiasm. It is more happy-go-lucky than the optimism of 3; a more complex influence that is sometimes astounding. Where a person influenced by number 3 is filled with self-confidence, the person influenced by 5 is usually indifferent to trouble and danger. The fearlessness of 5 does not recognize the existence of hazards; and the remarkable achievements of people of this vibration are often due to the fact that they can cope with an unexpected situation as easily as other persons can go about their daily tasks.

Number 5 brings a love of travel and a desire for new scenes. It is the great number of adventure; not adventure for the purpose of achievement, but adventure for the sake of adventure. It is a number of the wanderlust; and people who are typical examples of this number will undertake the strangest of enterprises. They are not inspired by the desire for conquest or fame; they are merely intrigued by the unusual and fascinated by the bizarre. They are ready for anything and will enter into projects where they play a secondary part simply because they desire new experience.

These people respond quickly; they are full of activity, and are always alert. They think out

effective and practical solutions of complex problems, and often amaze more conservative persons
by their unexpected courses of action.

Their faults are not few, and it is seldom that
a person of this number does not have a quota of
doubtful characteristics. Their desire for adventure leads them into foolish enterprises that may
bring them discredit. They do not care for consequences, and do not give proper thought to the
importance of affairs with which they are connected.

They sometimes become adventurers, and take
unfair advantage of other people; but it must be
said to their credit that they do not willingly try
to harm other people. While a person who has
the bad characteristics of number 1 may delib-
erately act unscrupulously to achieve a self-centered ambition, the individual controlled by 5 will
do a similar action through heedlessness. Some
of these people cannot appreciate the view-points
of other persons. They are so active and impul-
sive that they think everyone else is the same.

They live chiefly in the present; so they will
often begin many enterprises and will finish none.
Unlike people influenced by 3, they have little
regard for either the past or the future. Their
thirst for adventure is unquenchable. They have
a certain duality in their nature which is not difficult to analyze; for it is nothing more than the

changing from one activity to another. People influenced by number 5 are often considered eccentric by their friends; but those who truly understand them know that their desire for change is really responsible.

Thus a person influenced by number 5 may become quite successful in a certain profession, and may suddenly abandon it to take up a new business of a different occupation. People of more stable vibrations will look askance on such a course of action, wondering how anyone who has attained success in one direction will throw aside all the prestige that has been gained. The answer to this enigma is that number 5 carries a desire for activity, and an indifference toward attainment.

The desire for new scenes brings about a restlessness and a changeability in the nature of number 5. People who have this vibratory influence are often troubled by indecision. They will hesitate to embark upon a new channel because they feel that they may be committing themselves to a monotony of existence.

Furthermore, they are often influenced by a bad reaction. They become so interested in new surroundings that they forget past associations and neglect old friends. This brings them a great deal of unfair criticism which they do not rightfully deserve; for they are always glad and will-

ing to return to old scenes if they have a promise
of some new experiences.

They are very fond of social life, and make new
friends very easily. They enter into a new field
with great enthusiasm, and they often cause much
unhappiness when they suddenly depart from surroundings where they have made strong friendships.

They are successful in love, but will cast aside
an old sweetheart for a new one, and so they
are often considered to be faithless. But in real-
ity all their trouble is caused by the ease with
which they forget the past, and their lack of
thought for the future.

Number 5 is, however, so diversified in nature
that people coming under this vibration can develop themselves amazingly and may attain to
great heights if they can learn to modify some of
their natural characteristics. They will never
hope to be contented with a routine existence;
but they can gradually accustom themselves to
permanent surroundings and can learn to bring
adventure to themselves instead of constantly
seeking it.

They should try to use their talents to best
advantage; they should seek to find romance in
the commonplace. They should also endeavor to
make their active natures of benefit to mankind,

and should work for steadiness and singleness of purpose.

If they set their hearts upon gaining positive success in a definite field of action, and can content themselves by patiently waiting for excitement and adventure, they will soon realize that they possess characteristics that will prove of exceptional merit.

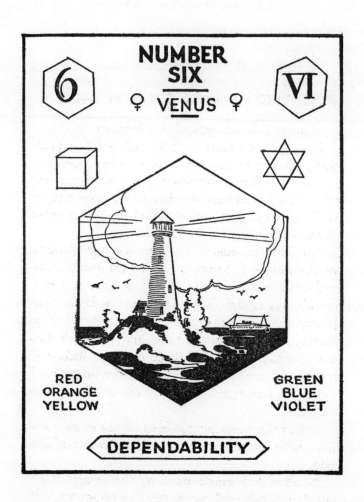

NUMBER
SIX
♀ __VENUS__ ♀

6

VI

RED
ORANGE
YELLOW

GREEN
BLUE
VIOLET

DEPENDABILITY

48

VIII. THE VIBRATION OF NUMBER 6

Number 6 is the symbol of Harmony.

It is the only number that combines the qualities of both odd and even. It is an even number, and it therefore possesses the characteristic stability of all even numbers, but at the same time it is divisible by three, and it therefore carries some of the brilliancy of that number.

Number 6 is, indeed, a harmonious combination of the numbers 2 and 3. It stands for balance and equilibrium, and at the same time it has a certain power that is progressive. It is the conjunction of two odd and equal numbers (two threes) to form a single even number; and it has also the triple union of three even and balanced numbers (three twos). It is the combination of inequality and equality, formed into a harmonious whole.

It has the material qualities of the even numbers, with a touch of the mental attributes of the odd.

Number 6 is represented by the hexagon; six sided, and balanced, yet perfect in symmetry. It is also symbolized by the six pointed star, which is formed by crossing of two triangles, significant of the number 3.

Its power of solidity is represented by the cube, which is six-sided. Thus it shows broader expansion than the square with its sign of 4. There are, also, six colors in the rainbow.

Much could be written about the number 6, for it is perhaps the most fortunate of all the numbers, and it is certainly the number whose characteristics are most equally distributed. It is stalwart and reliable, a most dependable number.

Number 6 is symbolized by the planet Venus, the bright luminary of the heavens, which represents goodness, truth, beauty, and love.

People who come under the vibratory influence of number 6 are reliable and honest. They revolt against all unscrupulous practices, and instinctively conform themselves to existing ideas of right and wrong. They are very conscientious, and hold truth to be the greatest of all virtues.

They are tolerant in disposition, and invariably seek out the true principles of any subject, holding up high ideals, and constantly striving to attain them. They are naturally unselfish, and peaceful in nature, but they will never fail to fight for the principles in which they believe.

They are not unreasonable in argument, although they generally feel that they are in the right. They form their own opinions with a real sense of impartiality, and so, even though they may not grant truth to another person's argument, they will give every subject fair consideration.

They are sometimes misled by mistaken ideals; but no matter in what course they may be led, they usually manage to modify their opinions so that they attain their natural level of kindliness.

Cheerfulness and optimism are present in the nature of number 6. Enthusiasm is lacking, but it is replaced by a quiet interest and a real belief that justice and honesty will surely prevail. This produces an evenness of disposition in people of this vibration, and it is a quality which stands in good stead.

The natural developments of number 6 are so excellent that there are very few faults to overcome; but no vibratory influence is perfect, and the people influenced by number 6 have their faults.

One of these bad qualities is caused by the presence of good qualities. There is a tendency for people of this vibration to feel that they are on a superior plane. Their natural sympathy toward other people sometimes changes to a sense of pity, and they begin to feel sorry for everyone else, taking the atttitude that if all other persons could attain their own degree of excellence, the world would be a paradise.

They sometimes become over-peaceful, and delude themselves with a foolish optimism, looking only at the desirable things of life, and comforting themselves with the mistaken notion that anything which is out of their sight or out of their minds does not exist. Thus they can destroy their greatest quality—that of natural sympathy; their willingness to be of help to others.

They are not selfish; but they often behave very selfishly because they have the false idea that they are doing the best thing they can.

Number 6 has natural possibilities toward the achievement of ambition; but the tendencies which have just been discussed often cause a person of this vibration to put aside ambition as being too worldly in nature. Many of these people are content to live quiet lives and to dwell in obscurity, helping a few people and feeling that they are thus performing a great life work. They do not realize that they are actually limiting their great power to do good, and are really behaving selfishly.

Two other faults of number 6 are poor business ability and a slight division of interests. People of this vibration generally feel that the end never justifies the means, and while they may be correct in their belief, they carry it to extremes, often refusing to identify themselves with causes in which they could do real good, simply because they are opposed to some minor matter that is really of no consequence.

Their division of interest, just mentioned, is not a marked tendency; but it consists of a very peculiar quality. A person of the vibratory influence of 6 may become interested in a certain project, and to that extent be of single purpose; but then, instead of centralizing effort in the cause or enterprise the person will try to develop it in many ways, following many blind courses, and paying too little attention to things that are really necessary.

The poor business ability often evidences itself in over-honesty, such as reticence to indulge in competition, and too much liberality toward persons who are undeserving of it.

People who have the vibration of 6 should seek to gain firmness and assertiveness. They are always capable of taking care of themselves, but they often delay too long before taking decisive action. They must be thoroughly aroused and grossly mistreated before they will assert themselves. They are, however, keen-minded enough to learn from experience, and after many unpleasant experiences they will usually adopt a more aggressive plan of action.

People who have this vibration have wonderful chances for success and very few faults to overcome. They are usually highly esteemed in the communities wherein they live, and in the proper environment they may attain great distinction. They are actively diplomatic, having the qualities of the numbers 2 and 3, and unless they are influenced by mistaken notions and let themselves lapse into passiveness they will surely succeed.

They do not, as a rule, gain great fame or become very wealthy, although such material success is within their power of attainment. They do not measure success by material standards, and when they do make money, they are generally philanthropic.

They should learn to develop the talents which they possess, and should seek to be of active aid to mankind, rather than resting in blissful contentment, feeling that they are doing their part in the world. Once they thoroughly realize that if they rise to high position and accumulate resources, they will be better able to help the world, they will be on the direct road to success and achievement.

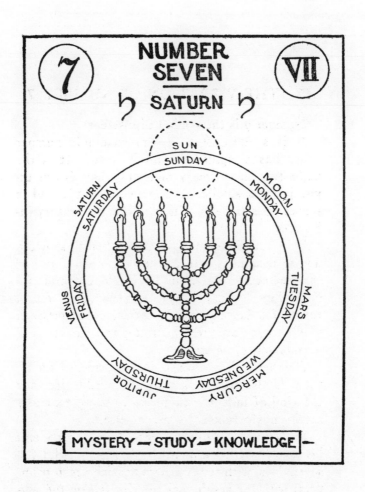

NUMBER
SEVEN

♄ SATURN ♄

7   VII

SUN
SUNDAY
SATURN SATURDAY
MOON MONDAY
VENUS FRIDAY
MARS TUESDAY
JUPITOR THURSDAY
MERCURY WEDNESDAY

➤ MYSTERY — STUDY — KNOWLEDGE ◄

IX. THE VIBRATION OF NUMBER 7

Number 7 is the symbol of mystery.

It is a deep, strange, unaccountable number which has a significance all its own. It is the highest of the primary numbers which is not divisible by a smaller number (except 1), and it shares no attributes with any other vibratory influences.

Since time immemorial, the number 7 has had a mystic meaning. It typifies a certain form of completeness, and despite its oddness and indivisibility it has always represented a certain form of balance; a single unit centered between two groups of three, forming an uneven but harmonious symmetry.

Number 7 has always been considered lucky; yet it is also to be taken as an unlucky sign, for the kind of luck it is supposed to bring generally carries misfortune for someone else.

In Biblical history we read how Joshua and his men marched around the city of Jericho for seven days, with seven priests bearing seven trumpets; with the result that the city fell on the seventh day after it had been encircled seven times.

There are many other remarkable stories involving the number 7, and it has always been significant of hiddden meaning.

The number stands for wisdom and perfection. There are seven major planets, seven notes in the scale, and seven days in the week.

But although the number 7 stands for wisdom, it is also significant of things which have been unexplained, and it is a number that has been greatly misunderstood.

It is symbolized by the planet Saturn, the dark, mysterious planet, which, with its mysterious rings, is different from all other heavenly bodies that constitute our solar system, and which is the planet of sinister meaning.

There are many good characteristics of the number 7; but they are all deep-seated and hidden from view. They are seldom understood or appreciated by the average person.

Studiousness and knowledge are evident in the number 7. People who have this vibration assimilate learning, and often develop a great store of wisdom. They turn their steps toward unexplored fields, and learn much that is little known.

There is inspiration in the number 7. It seems to carry a mystic key that brings a touch of the infinite, and an understanding of things beyond this world, however dim and imperfect that knowledge may be. It has been called the "psychic" number; but the true meaning of the word "psychic" is rather elusive. Numerology bears no relationship to spiritualistic phenomena, so the word "psychic" in this connection must be considered to mean mental as distinguished from physical and physiological.

Imagination is a notable attribute of the number 7. Persons in whom the vibration is particularly active will be highly imaginative, and many of them possess strange and uncanny mental powers.

There is certain poise also found under this number; an abstract dreaminess that cannot be imitated by persons who do not possess the vibration. The number 7 carries deep-set purpose, and it also is indicative of a peculiar type of valor; a mental courage that will prevail when physical bravery is lacking.

Number 7 is significant of Stoicism. People who possess its influence will undergo great hardships, and will combat terrible conditions without faltering.

Yet all of these qualities are little recognized. They are often known to the person who possesses them, yet not appreciated by other people. Most people who have these characteristics know of their presence, but merely accept them as a matter of course, and do not realize that they are powers or characteristics that are entirely unknown to the world at large.

Number 7 has its unfortunate side. It often produces great melancholy, and leads to gloominess and despair. The ordinary things of life seem shallow and commonplace to many people influenced by 7; and they yearn for higher, greater things, and feel discouraged because they realize that such things are beyond the power of human attainment.

With moodiness comes love of solitude. People who have this vibration enjoy quiet thought and retrospect. They like to weigh the affairs of life and human existence, and to imagine themselves beyond this earthly sphere. They are visionaries, and although they gain much because of their imaginative powers, they frequently become discontented with their surroundings.

Loneliness and unhappiness are often the lot of these people. They seek solitude; yet they cannot always have it. They must take some active interest in the usual affairs of the world, and when they give free rein to their peculiar, temperamental minds, they turn their lives into unnatural channels and find their desired existence in dreaming and inactivity; not in achievement.

Lack of self-expression is a great disadvantage found in the vibratory influence of number 7. A person of this type, finding himself misunderstood, seeks solace in solitude, and makes no effort to bring himself closer to those about him. Undevelopment is also an unfortunate characteristic of number 7. Many people who have real potentialities never manage to take advantage of their hidden possibilities.

There is one great requirement of the number 7. That is the bringing to the surface of all hidden powers. It is best accomplished by the formation of companionships, and the avoidance of too much solitude. It should be remembered, however, that the powers of number 7 are largely developed through quiet meditation, and such a practice should never be entirely discontinued. A person with the vibratory number of 7 should also be very careful to choose companions who will be real friends, ready to aid in the campaign of bringing out hidden ability.

An interest in the active affairs of life; an understanding of other people; and an application of knowledge in a practical way: these are the things which a person influenced by number 7 should seek to cultivate.

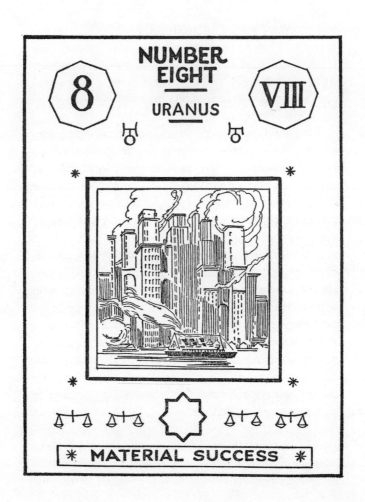

NUMBER EIGHT

URANUS

MATERIAL SUCCESS

X. THE VIBRATION OF NUMBER 8

Number 8 is the symbol of Material Progress. It has the equipoise of 2, and the solidity of 4; like its geometric representation, the octagon, it is many sided, but equally distributed. Like two squares placed together, it indicates a double strength; a power that is not satisfied with minor achievement.

Number 8 is the highest of the even primary numbers. It represents the ultimate in even construction, solid balanced regularity. Hence it allows no room for higher development. It lacks the quick brilliancy of the odd numbers, and does not possess imaginative qualities; but it is a great power in analysis and scientific understanding. It is broad, powerful and inclusive.

Number 8 combines the judgment of number 2 with the carefulness of number 4. It uses these two characteristics in a powerful manner, being governed by neither, and employing both to great advantage. It is like a strong, well-built, finished structure: perfect in material and capable of long endurance.

It is symbolized by the planet Uranus, which

stands for the Sun. Hence it has a common touch
with number 1, and possesses some of the determination and aggressiveness of that number; but
number 8, it must be remembered, does not possess either the inspiration or the quickness of purpose found in any of the odd numbers. It is not
a number of intuition.

Power is a characteristic that is evident in many
people who have the vibratory influence of number 8. They are capable of great achievements.
This number carries all the possibilities of material success. Those who have its vibration may
climb steadily to great heights in the world of
business and commerce.

They have the peculiar ability of building one
success upon another, so that they can expand
their projects and carry them beyond normal
limits. These people are stalwart, and never
wasteful of opportunity. They do not center all
their efforts upon a single line of effort as do the
adherents of number 1; instead of driving or
cutting their way through opposition, they over-
whelm it, and bring about alliances that all work
toward the final achievement.

Where number 1 depends upon cunning and
action, number 8 utilizes analysis and great practical knowledge. A person with this vibration
can always seem to think of some way whereby
he may strengthen his opportunities. He does not

rush forward blindly; nor does he fearlessly advance; instead, he moves slowly but steadily, studying every phase of the situation and gradually strengthening himself, until everything suddenly comes in his favor, as a natural result.

People with the vibratory influence of number 8 have great capabilities as executives. They not only know how to conduct their own affairs; they also know how to direct other people. They are not brilliant; they are practical-minded, and have uncommonly good sense. They take a constant interest in the affairs that confront them, and lead a life which is not imaginative, yet which is thoughtful of the future. They can quickly appreciate opportunities that lie before them, and they can easily induce other people to help them in their plans, because of the limited scope of vision of their associates.

They are not, however, unfair to other people. When anyone is of real assistance to them, they fit that person into their plans and see that he profits also. That is a great secret of their success; their ability to put every bit of mechanism into working order, and to maintain the maximum of efficiency. They are always working ahead of present plans, and are always thinking along constructive lines.

Self-assertiveness is one of their principal qualifications. They get what they want by sheer determination and strength of purpose, and they obtain their desires in such a way that they clear the path for continued progress.

They usually measure affairs in terms of material wealth; not because money is their one aim in life, but because they desire strength and power, and look upon wealth as a means of such achievement. They are never satisfied to become inactive after they have gained some material success, because the fruits of all their labors are always plucked after their plans have been well made, and their real desire lies in planning and execution. They often accept the results as a mere matter of course.

The number 8, therefore, means capacity for success and achievement. Yet not every one who possesses that vibratory number is successful. With some people, conditions do not permit of their plans reaching fulfillment. They may fail to overcome conflicts that arise between themselves and others of similar aptitude; or they may lack some important attribute that is necessary for success. It must be remembered that number 8 is a powerful, inclusive vibration; and it is very difficult to set it in motion. People who possess simpler vibratory numbers may develop their powers more easily.

There is another cause for lack of success among people who have the vibratory number of 8. That is the frequent presence of faults, or bad characteristics, which are difficult for the individual to realize, yet which may destroy the great power at his disposal.

The first fault, commonly found in all persons of this vibration, is lack of inspiration. This is generally replaced by forethought, a practical view of the future which is sometimes mistaken for inspiration. But number 8 never leaps forward to take a sweeping advantage, and there are times when such a course becomes absolutely necessary. As a result, persons of this type are restricted to a certain degree, and they are liable to fail unless they either have fortunate conditions before them, or develop a modicum of the necessary quality. Sometimes, the keen-minded person of number 8 vibration takes advantage of consultation with a person who possesses the traits which number 8 lacks, and wisely acts upon the advice given by another person.

Self-satisfaction is a bad characteristic of number 8. It sometimes causes the person of this vibration to depart from usual methods of procedure and to cease relying upon influences which seem trivial, yet which are really productive of results.

In a similar way, the self-assertiveness and executive ability of number 8 may gradually develop into domination. A lack of consideration for the interests of others will generally defeat

the aims of a person who has the vibration of 8;
for this number calls for coöperation. So when
a domineering tendency sets in, it may cause all
sorts of trouble. This is particularly true when
a person of number 8 is engaged in an enterprise
which involves a form of public service; for
domineering will cause enmities and will defeat
great powers of achievement.

There is another fault of number 8 that is
really dependent upon lack of inspiration. That
is over-success. When a person with the vibration of 8 has accomplished much, he will look forward to greater fields; and as long as his present
course of action opens the way for new achievement, he will progress. But once he has reached
the apex of attainment, he will lack imaginative
qualities that are necessary to new interests, and
will be forced to choose between speculative enterprises or inactivity. Either course may lead to
decay and dissolution. Many persons who have
attained much have lost it either through hazardous undertakings or through inability to remain
progressive after they have established themselves.

Singularly enough, number 8 is a power for re-
construction. The ability is lacking to recuper-
ate after a well-established life work has gradually disintegrated, for number 8 must be always
progressive and does not ordinarily "come back."

But 8 is positively unequalled when it comes to taking the affair of others and putting them on a sound, remunerative basis: That is because number 8 knows how to organize and strengthen; and the services of a person of this vibration have often been instrumental in building up interests or enterprises that have just barely managed to exist.

The tendency of number 8 toward domination also leads to waywardness and that may prove to be a dangerous fault. As long as a person of this vibratory influence keeps actively engaged in constructive progress, matters will take care of themselves; but if temporary achievement proves misleading, there is always the danger that the person will gradually change his course of action, and will develop a false purpose. Number 8 seldom indicates sudden change; hence the transition from an effective plan of action to a faulty one is never realized by the individual himself.

Number 8 is complete in itself; attainment is its natural heritage. Where other numbers represent striving toward a distant and intangible goal, number 8 stands for natural completion. Sensible, practical conduct will always lead to attainment; but the important thing to remember is that the entirety and completeness of number 8 must be preserved. Some people who have this vibratory influence do not realize the great power for success which is at their disposal.

One requirement needed by people of this vibration is that of thoughtfulness. They should seek to realize that there are many sides to life, and that the dreamer and the student have a goal which is just as high as that of wealth and power.

They should desire variety of interests, and should try to interest themselves in things that are not restricted to business. By broadening their vision, and finding pleasure in diversion, they can create a sense of enthusiasm which will place them in close contact with human existence; and thus they will attain a point of view that will safeguard them from the injurious faults which so often beset this number.

If they retain their desire to progress along certain lines, but do not lay too much emphasis upon wealth and power, they will gain great enjoyment from their success, and will be able to live happily after their active attainments have been consummated.

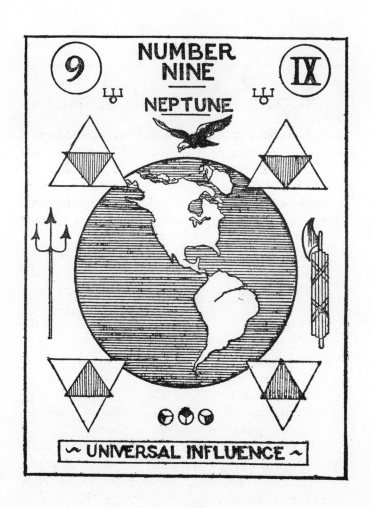

XI. THE VIBRATION OF NUMBER 9

Number 9 is the symbol of Universal Influence. It is a number of perfection, the triune of triplicity. It is complete and powerful, like the number 8; but it has not direct connection with material gain. It is the number of regeneration, and stands for a high state of mental and spiritual development.

The greatest of all the primary numbers, 9 is capable of many things. It has a certain mystic significance, and it is a number that brings great achievement.

Number 9 is typified by universal love; not the placid, quiet love of number 6; but a magnetic, far-reaching love; a desire to benefit humanity in practical, active ways.

It combines certain attributes of all other numbers, and its vibratory influence can become harmonious, powerful, and ever existent. It is a number of great idealism, and mighty ambition.

Number 9 is symbolized by the planet Neptune. Number 9 is unlike the changeable, delicate number 2 which stands for the Moon, but it does draw a certain tendency for indecision, which is sometimes noticeable among the wide range of characteristics which are present in this number.

Knowledge is a great attribute of 9. People who have this number are often very intelligent; and they do not apply their learning along any specific channel. They grasp facts quickly; yet they are also inclined to studiousness. They do not lay too much importance upon practical knowledge, but they gain their share of it; on the other hand, they find an interest in abstract learning, but do not permit themselves to be carried away by it.

They are artistic in nature, have charming personalities, possess talent, and have dramatic ability. They are outstanding, and often develop a high personality that is greatly admired.

There is something about the highly developed influence of number 9 that inspires the confidence of other people. Those who have the vibration of 9 will often find themselves successful and appreciated, without the necessity of great effort. They will easily gain results where others have failed, simply because they have natural qualifications that constantly appear on the surface, and are recognized as underlying traits.

People who have this number are keen thinkers. They store up knowledge through natural ability; and do not look upon learning as the only key to happiness or fame. With them, such matters are accepted as part of the ordinary work of life.

And so, the vibratory influence of 9 brings power of understanding, a real appreciation of human nature, and a sympathetic touch with life that is spontaneous and ever present.

Integrity is another good quality of the powerful number 9. People of this influence do not draw fine distinctions, and set a great value upon truth and honesty, as do the adherents of number 6. They have their high ideals and their sense of honesty as a natural, spontaneous inclination, and they regard it as a logical course of conduct, without analyzing the subject. In other words, where number 6 exalts honesty and loves to compare its goodness with the baseness of dishonesty, number 9 makes no comparisons, but gives honesty and expects the same return.

In our system of notation number 9 is number 6 inverted. In Numerology, the mere symbols of numbers have no significance; but it is a strange coincidence to note that the two numbers 6 and 9 are almost identical in form, yet exactly opposite in interpretation. The oddness of 9 contrasts with the evenness of 6, although 6 has certain qualities of the odd numbers, due to its formation of two threes. But the exactitude of 6 is not found in 9. All the preciseness and careful choice of the former number is replaced by spontaneous action in the latter. Thus the vibratory influences of the two numbers produce great differences in the individuals who come under them.

Number 9 has its faults. With it, ambition always seems easy to gratify; and so the person who has this influence is apt to defer constructive action, always feeling that he can utilize it when occasion demands. This leads to the loss of many possible achievements.

Dreaminess and lack of concentration are two other faults. There is inspiration in the number 9—plenty of it; but a person generally applies it in a broad, vague way, finding romance and harmony in everything, and seeking the beautiful in life to so great an extent that active work is relegated to odd moments.

Just as number 7 produces a melancholy dreaminess, so does number 9 bring about a mental enjoyment of nature, a joyous contemplation of the things of the world.

If the person who experiences these meditative pleasures can but catch the fleeting thoughts and apply them to the benefit of himself and mankind, he will profit greatly because of his vibratory influence of 9; but, unfortunately, this is not often done. Where the dreams of number 7 are haunting, powerful and so realistic that they finally force action and demand recognition, the visions of 9 are intangible, rosy, and vague, and they lose their lustre when analyzed.

The lack of concentration comes with the phase of dreaminess. A person influenced by number 9 will often set out upon a specific course of reasoning, and will gradually drift away from the goal. This is probably due to the general knowledge gained by the vibration of 9; a knowledge which loves to find points of similarity in affairs which are entirely different, and which takes pleasure in balancing and comparing things.

Impractical ideas are also the lot of number 9. This comes of a desire to put certain dreams or visions into action, with an effort, at the same time, to maintain their idealism. Number 9 is not impractical in application, and a person of this vibration soon realizes the faults of an idea which seemed remarkable in its conception.

The number 9 is capable of the highest development, for it can be made all-inclusive, and it may prove to be a great power in the world. The needed requirements are application, forethought, and commercial sense.

As number 9 is not impractical in application, a person of this vibration should begin by strengthening that quality. Application is not ordinarily present, and if it is stimulated, it will be successful. Therefore it is the line of the least resistance in the development of this vibratory influence.

Forethought often comes as a result of concentrated application. That is seen in the high development of the number 8. Number 9 should profit thereby, and seek to cultivate the needed requirement.

Similarly, commercial sense is present in number 8, which possesses application and forethought. Number 9 can attain this quality in the course of time; but application and forethought do not necessarily develop commercial sense.

In fact, number 9 seldom makes the material progress gained by number 8, except as the indirect result of other attainment. Yet number 9 is significant of power, and if its good qualities are hightly developed, the person of this vibration may gain influence and power that all the wealth of number 8 could never buy.

XII. THE CONFLICTS AND HARMONIES
OF NUMBERS

Each number has its influence upon every other number.

Certain numbers combine effectively; others, like oil and water, do not mix.

As every person is under the vibratory influence of more than one number, it is advisable that he should know whether or not his vibrations are conflicting or harmonious. However, each vibration in the individual is somewhat independent, finding its own fulfillment in its proper place. When one person meets another, there is the possibility of comparing two vibratory numbers that have the same realization. Hence the conflict and harmonies of numbers have a real importance.

The following list of vibratory numbers is simply an outline, giving brief facts regarding the combined interpretations of numbers.

Number 1 is powerful, but narrow, when combined with 1.

Number 1 gives decision, but may cause trouble with 2.

Number 1 is helpful rather than injurious to number 3.

Number 1 is strengthening and valuable to number 4.

Number 1 is helpful but does not greatly affect 5.

Number 1 is good, but not properly understood with 6.

Number 1 is troublesome in combination with number 7.

Number 1 is powerful in combination with number 8.

Number 1 is strengthening, but is absorbed by 9.

Number 2 is an excellent modifier of number 1.

Number 2 is weak and vacillating with number 2.

Number 2 has little effect upon number 3.

Number 2 forms an integral part and is helpful to 4.

Number 2 disagrees strongly with and is troublesome to 5.

Number 2 is easily absorbed and is of value to 6.

Number 2 is well understood, but is not strengthening to 7.

Number 2 is of very little importance to number 8.

Number 2 is harmonious, but slightly weakening to 9.

Number 3 gives greater scope to number 1.

Number 3 is understood by, and gives activity to 2.

Number 3 is quite effective with number 3.

Number 3 is a helpful influence to number 4.

Number 3 is effective with both numbers 5 and 6.

Number 3 has points of agreement with number 7.

Number 3 is apt to be inharmonious with number 8.

Number 3 is especially effective with number 9.

Number 4 gives development to numbers 1, 8, and 9.

Number 4 restrains and belittles number 2.

Number 4 gives needed strength to number 3.

Number 4 is very slow and clumsy with number 4.

Number 4 should help but is usually not accepted by 5.

Number 4 is not helpful to number 6.

Number 4 often prevents the development of 7.

Number 5 broadens the scope and activity of number 1.

Number 5 gives foolish impulses to number 2.

Number 5 is of value to numbers 3 and 9.

Number 5 causes trouble for number 4.

Number 5 produces power but lack of purpose with 5.

Number 5 enlivens but sometimes retards 6.

Number 5 develops the less desirable traits of 7.

Number 5 causes lack of balance in number 8.

Number 6 is a good, stable influence with numbers 1, 3, and 8.

Number 6 does not give impetus to but it does help 2.

Number 6 brings contentment but not vision to 4.

Number 6 modifies the ceaseless activity of 5.

Number 6 is harmonious but rather placid with 6.

Number 6 assists in the development of numbers 7 and 9.

Number 7 gives depth but not broadness to number 1.

Number 7 adds vision but not action to number 2.

Number 7 often proves of great value to number 3.

Number 7 brings happiness to number 4.

Number 7 has a peculiar and uncertain influence on 5 and 6.

Number 7 is often melancholy and unfortunate with 7.

Number 7 should be helpful but is not understood by 8.

Number 7 is valuable and easily absorbed but restraining 9.

Number 8 gives power but not scruples to 1.

Number 8 gives material potentialities to 2 and 4.

Number 8 is doubtful but sometimes valuable to 3 and 5.

Number 8 often proves of inestimable value to 6.

Number 8 strives to help but is seldom understood by 7.

Number 8 is too complete when combined with 8.

Number 8 gives great chances for success to number 9.

Number 9 broadens and enlightens number 1.

Number 9 steadies but has too much similarity to 2.

Number 9 gives great powers of achievement to 3 and 4.

Number 9 is a helpful but not permanent influence on 5.

Number 9 is extremely useful and harmonious to 6.

Number 9 reduces melancholy but does not thoroughly enliven 7.

Number 9 gives inspiration and power to number 8.

Number 9 is very strong, but too diversified with 9.

Note: It will be seen that in the above tables, the effect of the first number named is given on the second number. Thus one number may help another, but may not receive a fair return for its efforts.

There are two specific ways in which the conflicts and harmonies of numbers may be studied to good purpose.

(1) In the choosing of business associates.

(2) In consideration of love and matrimony.

Under the first heading, the characteristics of the numbers should follow the table rather closely; but in ascertaining whether or not two people will harmonize in business, their *Numbers of Development* should be compared. No other numbers have any particular significance in conflict and harmony, where enterprise is concerned.

In the matter of matrimony, the *Birth Numbers* are the ones that are significant. The same is true in the choice of friends. That is why business often fails when built upon friendship; and also why friendship does not always result from close business association.

Friendship and love are instinctive, based upon a mutual attraction, in which the deeper traits, those of the Birth Number, predominate.

Business is built upon usefulness, and coöperation. It is a more formal relationship, and is a different sphere of activity.

No one should, however, look upon any of these rules as iron-clad. There is always the possibility of a hidden trait, a peculiarity of genius or disposition that may alter circumstances.

Numerology cannot be gauged by individuals, for it is of broad scope and deals with general indications, not in specific instances, although many of them may be cited as remarkable examples.

The whole point is this: Numerology can be and has been used to advantage in the study of characteristics, self-development, and the choice of friends and business associates. It is not difficult to discover an instance in which the general rules have not operated exactly as expected; but on the contrary, many cases may be found where everything has run true to form. If these are attributed to coincidence, the others should be also.

The real purpose of this chapter, as of every other chapter in the book is to expound the possibilities of Numerology and its universal interpretation according to rules that have survived the test of time. The person who uses these indications wisely, and to good advantage, will surely profit from them.

XIII. THE SECONDARY NUMBERS AND THEIR SIGNIFICANCE

According to an ancient system, every number from 1 to 22 inclusive has an especial value, this being due to the fact that there were twenty-two mystic letters in the Hebrew alphabet.

As will be explained in the following chapters, a number between 10 and 22 is frequently encountered before the number of a date or a name has been reduced to one of the important primary numbers.

For example, March 5, 1900 consists of the figures 3, 5, 1, 9, 0, 0, which total 18. The figures 1 and 8 total 9, which is the primary number influencing that date. But the number 18 has been encountered on the way.

Similarly, as will later be explained, the letters in the name Ian Hay have a total value of 17, which reduces to 8, the sum of 1 and 7. And 17 has been encountered before the primary number has been attained.

Such would not be the case in a name or date with a number value of 26, for in that case, the primary number would reduce to 8, the sum of

2 and 6, without involving any secondary number.

Some persons have endeavored to attribute a special value to the secondary numbers 11 and 22, classifying them with the primary numbers. But this is a mistake, for 11 reduces to 2 and 22 reduces to 4. A great many numbers encounter 11 while being reduced to 2, and if 11 were given a powerful individual significance, the indications would be out of proportion to the actual results. The indications of secondary numbers are spasmodic and uncertain. They cannot be relied upon, and many false impressions have been created through over-emphasis of the values of 11 and 22. These numbers are somewhat more powerful than the other secondary numbers, but they do not in any case alter the existing vibration of the primary number. They merely supplement it with hidden, deep-set possibilities which occasionally come to the surface in the individual, and which are often of temporary duration. They are elusive and difficult to develop or modify, as their existence is not always certain.

The values of the secondary numbers are as follows:

10.—A number that signifies completion, being one greater than the number 9; but having no important value as the only tangible number which appears in it is the number 1, to which 10 is reduced. It has no practical value.

11.—A number that indicates possible genius. It stands for imagination and temperament; but it functions only in exceptional cases. Should it occur more than once in the Numerology of an individual, it will be more likely to have influence; but ordinarily it is of no value, and usually resolves itself into the number 2 without giving any added significance.

12.—This number usually resolves quietly into 3. If it appears twice in a Numerology, or if its single appearance happens to carry influence, it will indicate a sense of balance that simulates the number 6. On the contrary, it may be an agency of restraint that will cause misfortune and restrain development.

13.—This is an unfortunate number that signifies disappointment, disaster and misfortune. It is not over-active, however, and is usually avoided. As it reduces to the number 4, it is probably because of its influence that 4 has been misinterpreted to be the number of misfortune. The blame in most cases can be traced back to 13.

14.—This number is a good one; being twice 7, it carries some of the intellectual characteristics of that number, balanced and harmonized. Hence 14 often adds needed qualities to the uncertain characteristics of number 5.

15.—This is a number that carries willfulness, and leads often to bad results. It is the influence which sometimes injures the virtues of number 6, so it should be carefully watched.

16.—This number is a symbol of pride, and like pride, it goes before a fall. It bears indications of overthrow and calamity, and it makes the development of number 7 a difficult task.

17.—This is a strong, helpful number that gives assurance and confidence whenever it appears. It is indicative of high success, and often proves to be an excellent addition to number 8, to which it reduces. It is often responsible for the success and development of number 8.

18.—This is a doubtful, uncertain number; but its influence is frequently lacking. It is symbolic of darkness and gloom, two elements which are harmful to the development of number 9. It occasionally produces in a person influenced by 9 peculiar characteristics that are similar to the melancholy traits of number 7, and it is the cause of certain outstanding exceptions to the rules of 9.

19.—This is a powerful, brilliant number, a symbol of the Sun. It carries the progressiveness of number 1 and also the inclusiveness of the number 9. It reduces to 10, and then to 1, and it gives great opportunities to its possessors.

20.—This is a number that reduces to 2. It aids in the development of a passive nature, bringing out strengthening influences, but in a moderate way. It may, if repeated, signify accomplishment. Its power, however, is not outstanding, and unless it is utilized, it will gradually disappear. A great many persons, influenced by number 2, have never developed themselves because they have neglected the possibilties brought through number 20. This number will never work for itself. It is strengthening, but of a passive nature, obscure and not easy to appreciate.

21.—This is a number that indicates steadfastness. It does not carry balance, but it adds potentialities to number 3, and makes itself evident as soon as that number is developed. It is a stepping-stone to achievement that will readily be active as soon as the possessor of it becomes active and progressive.

22.—This is a strange, intangible number that has a mysterious influence. It is a difficult number to analyze, for it seems to be partly hidden in the obscure shadows of the higher, non-influential numbers. It can never be controlled, and it is seldom active; but once it takes effect it will either bring phenomenal success or will produce folly and privation. We cannot study it for causes; we can merely attribute results to its presence.

This concludes the secondary numbers, and it should be remembered that their importance is really secondary. The simple vibrations of the primary numbers 1 to 9 are the real essence of Numerology; and it is their very simplicity that makes the study of this science so effective. The secondary numbers should be regarded as purely incidental, representing possibilities that are comparatively remote, and having none of the recognized probability found in the primary numbers.

The great majority of people will have noticeable characteristics which conform to their primary numbers of vibration. The purpose of the secondary numbers is to classify some of the exceptional cases and to explain the presence or absence of particular attributes.

The study of Numerology would be valuable and highly satisfactory if the primary numbers and their important vibrations alone were considered. There are many minor developments of Numerology, some of which have not been correctly analyzed; these represent an expansion of the fundamental principles, and the study of the secondary numbers is one of the ramifications which has been well established. So the reputed significance of those numbers has been given in this chapter for the purpose of completeness and information to the reader who may be interested in them; but no one should attempt to compare them with the primary numbers.

XIV. THE BIRTH NUMBER AND THE NAME NUMBER

There are two numbers that form a foundation in the career of every individual. They do not depend upon the interpretation of letters, which give deeper insight into the characteristics of the person; but they do form the basis for preliminary calculation.

The first of these is called the "Birth Number."

It represents the primary status of the individual. Its significance is similar to that of an astrological calculation; for it is nothing more nor less than the reduction to figures of the date of a person's birth.

Scientists explain that heredity and environment are the two great governing influences of life. Birth represents the transition from the influence of heredity to that of environment. It is possible, through Numerology, to classify the mathematical powers of heredity and environment; and, in the same way, the Birth Number may be determined.

There are nine vibrating numbers; and every person, at birth, immediately assumes one of those numbers. The Birth Number is ascertained by simply adding the figures that compose the month, the day and the year of birth, and reducing them to one of the key numbers of Numerology.

Each month carries the number of its position upon the calendar. January = 1; February = 2; March = 3; April = 4; May = 5; June = 6; July = 7; August = 8; September = 9; October = 10; November = 11; December = 12.

The days of the month carry their own numbers; and each year has its particular number.

Thus, a person born upon the first of January, 1900, would have the following numerical representation: 1—1—1900. By adding the figures 1, 1, 1, 9, 0, 0, a total of 12 is gained. To reduce 12 to a key number, simply add 1 and 2, giving 3 as the key number, or number of vibration.

Taking as an example a child born on December 19, 1926, the representation would be 12—19—1926; the figures 1, 2, 1, 9, 1, 9, 2, 6 add up to 31. The figures 3 and 1 reduce to the key number 4.

The birthday of the seventh of May, 1899 becomes 5—7—1899. The figures 5, 7, 1, 8, 9, 9 total 39. 3 and 9 make 12; and 1 and 2 total 3, forming 3 as the key number of the individual born on that date.

According to this arrangement, it will be seen

that every person born on one particular day will have the same Birth Number. This does not mean that two persons with the same birthday will be identical or very similar in characteristics. It does, however, signify that they will have a mutual interest, in that their respective life-journeys begin at the same time. The Birth Number, moreover, does not reveal all characteristics; it really signifies the conditions of the world, humanity and nature that should exist at that particular period. In infancy, a person is governed entirely by other persons; and just as a baby grows and develops self-reliance, depending less and less upon the help of others, so does the individual gradually come under the influence of the higher branches of Numerology.

But with it all, the Birth Number still remains, and is a primary factor throughout life. No man can change his birthday; it is decreed and established; and the Birth Number is the Numerological symbol of the birthday.

A slight and minor influence is the "Name Number."

A name is similar to a birthday; for each person receives his or her name, without having any choice in the matter. Here, however, the individual can alter circumstances; for it is quite possible to change a name, even though a birthday must always remain the same.

But it is beyond the power of any human being to alter events which have passed; and the months or years during which a person has had a certain name can never be obliterated. So, in conjunction with the Birth Number, we have the Name Number, which is derived from the name bestowed upon a child and actually chosen and registered as the name of the individual.

To find the Numerological value of the name, and its influence in childhood, simply add up the number of letters, and reduce the total to a key number.

Thus: JOHN WILLIAM WALLACE.

There are 18 letters in the name, and the figures 1 and 8 total 9. So 9 is the Name Number of John William Wallace, and it represents the vibratory influence that will exist in the infancy and early childhood of the person who bears that name.

But here we have a different matter to consider. While the Birth Number remains constant and unchanging, and always exerts a certain subtle influence throughout life; the Name Number undergoes a process of greater development that gives an insight into the characteristics, capabilities, and progress of the person.

To a young child, a name means nothing; to an older person, it is a matter of great importance. Personalities, achievements, and ideals are all associated with names.   When we speak of a person's name, we mean *names;* because each person's name consists of two or more separate names.   Just as people possess composite names, so do they possess composite personalities.   Each name has its own importance, and its own vibratory number, and these will be explained in the next chapter.

XV. THE NUMBER OF YOUR NAME

Active—Passive—Hereditary—Destiny

Each letter of the alphabet has its own special number, in accordance with recognized tables, or a Kabbala of Numbers.

The exact numerical value of each letter may vary according to the particular system employed. A very simple unit value has been made up from the English alphabet; but the use of numbers to stand for letters goes back beyond the origin of our alphabet. A table may be formed from the Greek alphabet; there is another form of letter values attributed to Pythagoras; and further systems exist.

It is a well-known fact that the Hebrew alphabet, and writings in that tongue abound in mystical meanings. The Kabbala itself is of Hebrew origin, based upon the letters of the Jewish alphabet; so in the study of Numerology the most reliable system to adopt is the one that transcribes the meanings of Hebrew letters into the English alphabet; for the modern alphabet was not prepared with any direct reference to the significance of numbers.

98

There is no need to explain just why each letter has its special number; for the purpose of this book is to enable the reader to use Numerology as a practical form of knowledge.

The table of the alphabet with values in numbers is as follows:

A = 1	J = 1	S = 3
B = 2	K = 2	T = 4
C = 2	L = 3	U = 6
D = 4	M = 4	V = 6
E = 5	N = 5	W = 6
F = 8	O = 7	X = 6
G = 3	P = 8	Y = 1
H = 8	Q = 1	Z = 7
I = 1	R = 2	TH = 9 * PH = 8 *

With the letters and their numerical values at our disposal, it is a simple matter to find the key numbers of persons' names.

Take for example, the name given in the last chapter: John William Wallace.

J = 1	W = 6	W = 6
O = 7	I = 1	A = 1
H = 8	L = 3	L = 3
N = 5	L = 3	L = 3
	I = 1	A = 1
	A = 1	C = 2
	M = 4	E = 5
——	——	——
21	19	21

*The digraph "th" comes from the Hebrew letter Teth, which corresponds to the Greek letter Theta. The Anglo-Saxon

The vibratory number of JOHN is 3, found by adding 2 and 1.

The vibratory number of WILLIAM is 1; for 9 and 1 make 10; and 1 and 0 total 1.

The vibratory number of WALLACE is 3; the sum of 2 and 1.

The vibratory number of the *entire name* is 7; 3 plus 1 plus 3. It may also be gained by adding 21 plus 19 plus 21, total 61, and then reducing 6 and 1 to 7.

The number of the entire name is of great importance; for it is the Number of Destiny, or the Number of Fate, the first definite vibration that affects the individual. It is a mark of individuality that distinguishes him from others who have the same Birth Number; it is the groundwork upon which he may build his future.

Now the Number of Destiny has its Numerological factors. They are the numbers of the single names. The letters and their values may be likened to fractions, the single names to integers, and the entire name to a multiple.

The last name, the family name, is called the hereditary name, and carries the Hereditary Number. In this case it is 3. It indicates hereditary characteristics of the individual; it is a

language, with the letters "edh" and "thorn" had the equivalent of "th," which should, accordingly, be given the value of 9 in the table. Ph is given the value of F.

name which he possesses in common with other members of his family; and it represents tendencies which have accumulated through past generations.

The first name is the active name, and it carries the Active Number. It points out certain qualities of the individual, and forms the basis of personal activities. If, however, a person commonly uses his middle name from childhood on, it will become the Active Name, and the subordinated first name will take a passive place.

The middle name (or the subordinated first name) is the passive name. Its Passive Number carries very little influence, and it is often demoted to a mere initial. It serves, however, as a sort of connecting link between the hereditary name and the active name. Often a person's middle name is an old family name, frequently the maiden name of a mother. In such cases, the passive name virtually becomes a hereditary name.

Some persons have four, five, or even more names. In such cases the Passive Names are of very little importance, for they are greatly divided. If, however, one such name stands out more prominently than the other, it has greater significance. The best plan, however, is to add up all the passive names and treat them as one.

Sometimes a child's name is changed by its

parents, before the child has learned its own name. In such instances the new name is the one to be considered in Numerology; for the present discussion deals with names that have come into recognized use.

These three types of names are the component parts of the entire name, with its Number of Destiny. They account for differences in individuals who have the same Number of Destiny. Each one has a slight vibratory influence, which may sometimes be used to a great extent.

For instance, a person with Active, Passive and Hereditary Numbers 3, 6, and 7 will have a total of 16, making 7 the Number of Destiny. Another person, with 2, 5, and 9, will also have a total of 16, with 7 as the Number of Destiny. These two persons will be governed by the same complete vibration; yet each one will have underlying vibratory influences that are entirely different.

The *Number of Destiny* requires important attention; for it represents the completed whole —a certain, definite vibration which is certain to show visible effects. It stands for the primary characteristics of the individual as they first manifest themselves in life; an influence which should be studied carefully, and with which future actions should be harmonized, according to the application of Numerology.

The lesser names point out possible ways in which the Number of Destiny may be developed. They give a clue to the construction of that important number.

Following the Number of Destiny comes the Number of Development, which is discussed at length in the next chapter. It is based upon the adopted name, which is explained as follows:

Few people use their names in full form. Thus John William Wallace is likely to call himself John W. Wallace, J. William Wallace, or J. W. Wallace; or he may go under the name of John Wallace or William Wallace.

John William Wallace has 7 as his Number of Destiny, its component parts being 3, 1, and 3. If he uses the name John W. Wallace, he will gradually assume characteristics of the number 3, which is found by adding and reducing the values of the letters in John W. Wallace.

As J. William Wallace, his new vibratory number will be 5. As J. W. Wallace, it will be 1.

John Wallace, as a name, produces the vibratory number 6. William Wallace produces the vibratory number 4.

Therefore, in adopting a logical, normal name for everyday use, John William Wallace may choose the vibratory influence of 3, 5, 1, 6, or 4, unless he decides to preserve his full name and thus foster 8 as his Number of Development.

He should, of course, choose a name that will be in harmony with his Number of Destiny.

Some people never adopt a definite name. This man, for example, might write under the name of John William Wallace, conduct his business as John W. Wallace, and keep a bank account in the name of J. W. Wallace. Such a plan of action would virtually eliminate the Number of Development, because there would be no true and definite adopted name. If one name could be chosen as possessing greatest importance, it would have potentiality; otherwise the individual would gain certain qualities of each new vibratory influence; but only to a small degree. He could hardly hope to achieve any of the benefits of any one of those numbers, and he would be liable to encounter some of their undesirable characteristics. Success and achievement are only attainable through concentrated effort and definiteness of purpose.

As a groundwork for further consideration we may summarize the importance of the numbers of names as follows:

THE NUMBER OF DESTINY.—A guiding influence of life; the summary of individuality; the indicative number of probable position and progress that is of great importance in the training of childhood and youth.

The Active Number.—Personal relationship

and friendships; certain minor traits of individuality.

The Passive Number.—Occasional characteristics; but only a modifying influence, and then very slight.

The Hereditary Number.—Inherited characteristics; family similarities.

THE NUMBER OF DEVELOPMENT.—The surface number; an assumed personality; a new channel which may be developed through life; the opportunity for individual activity, indicating failure, success, or departure from ordinary and restrictive conditions.

Of those which have been elucidated in this chapter, the entire name, which produces the Number of Destiny, is by far the most important. The other three: Active, Passive, and Hereditary, are but minor influences, weak and incomplete.

The entire name is a finished thing, moulding together all the potentialities of the others; for it is the sum of the three minor names, and it is really of consequence.

Bear this fact in mind, for it is important. The various names of the individual are but the elements that compose the great atmosphere of life. They are like hydrogen, oxygen and nitrogen, each a separate substance that goes into the forming of air. Just as human beings require air, so do they come under the vibratory influence of the Number of Destiny, which is universal and greatly important, gained from the grand total of the names of which it is composed.

XVI. THE ADOPTED NAME

THE NUMBER OF DEVELOPMENT

First impressions are of considerable importance in life. We often form our opinions of people after seeing them once only. Very few persons possess the ability to analyze another person quickly; and that is why so many friendships are short-lived, and so many prejudices are formed.

Sometimes we form friendship with people whom we have never seen, through the medium of correspondence. In these days of modern inventions, it is possible to listen to the voice of a person without seeing him; and the listener invariably receives a mental impression of the speaker.

Furthermore, there is the case of celebrities: persons whom we neither see, hear, nor correspond with yet who are of interest in our lives. We customarily like or dislike such people and build up mental impressions of their characteristics that are based purely upon hearsay.

If a person will go over a list of people who are

of interest to him in his daily life, he will probably discover that he *really knows* a very small
proportion of them. If he goes further, and attempts to classify them under the heads of different types, he will find that he has a place for
nearly everyone he is acquainted with or has met
or corresponded with; yet he, in putting them
where he thinks they belong, is basing his judgment not upon an exact analysis, but upon his own
impressions; his own likes or dislikes; and his own
standards of excellence or his own prejudices!

Now there are two important things that we
remember about every person we meet. One is
appearance; the other is name. Under the head
of appearance we have facial characteristics, man-
nerisms, voice, carriage, dress, and other clues to
character. *All these* are on one side of the
balance; *the name* is on the other.

This proves that a name is a matter of great
significance.

We may see a man every day, and never speak
to him or make his acquaintance. He will mean
no more to us than a mere name in a newspaper
paragraph. Yet we may hear of a person—of his
name only—and feel a real sense of acquaintanceship.

The name by which we know so many people is
the *name of adoption*. We unconsciously form
opinions of characteristics through knowledge of

the name alone, and as each name can be reduced to a fundamental vibratory number, that number is going to have a great deal to do with the impressions given out by the name. It makes no difference whether a person knows anything about Numerology or not. The name creates its prestige, and the name has its fundamental number. Upon this basis we can establish the following rule:

The name of adoption, with its Number of Development, is the influence which creates first impressions in the minds of other persons.

From this, we come logically to another rule of equal importance, namely:

The importance of the Number of Development increases proportionately with the increase of acquaintanceship, fame, or prominence of the individual.

This enables us to realize the significance of stage names, pen names, and fictitious names.

To his family, close friends, and relations, a man is known by his full and original name. To be sure, they may call him by a nickname; or they may never use his middle name among themselves; but they are all familiar with his full name, and should any of them decide to analyze his name according to Numerology, they would logically take his full name as a working basis.

As the man progresses in life, and uses his

adopted name exclusively, the majority of people who meet him or hear of him, will know him by his adopted name alone. His middle name may be Thompson; but the letter T will take its place in everyday life, and to the great majority of persons it will represent his middle name. If a chance acquaintance should undertake to analyze the man's Numerology, he would have to use the letter T alone instead of the full name Thompson. So, in this case, the name of adoption would produce a vibratory number which would truly be a Number of Development.

When an adopted name has reached its new status gradually, it represents a natural course of development. It will slowly supersede the old name; therefore, the new vibratory number must be considered with the old one—the Number of Destiny; but if those numbers do not naturally harmonize, the result will not be serious, because of the natural course of development. On the contrary, if the numbers do harmonize, there will be no startling advance or sudden development in the individual.

But suppose the person changes his name entirely. Then he is apt to cause a real conflict if his two numbers do not harmonize. To many people he will be known by his old name; and at first his new name will fit him like a poorly made garment.

As he develops his new name, he may succeed

in eradicating almost all the influence of the old one; but if he has attempted too drastic a change, and has made it after his old name has been firmly established, the influence of the old name will remain, and the new one will be but an empty shell, without any worth-while meaning.

A pen name or a stage name presents another phase of the situation. In some cases it marks a real change in the career of the person who adopts it; but more often it does nothing more than assist in creating an illusive impression upon the people who become familiar with it.

Many persons read novels and think of the author as a man representing the type of characters he creates, whereas in private life he is entirely different. Movie fans look upon certain actors as their ideals and think of them as really being the romantic figures that they portray on the screen. So it is with the names of actors and authors; they may be nothing more than a rôle; and their vibratory numbers may have no significance at all.

There are, however, actors and authors who base their work upon their own personality, and really live their lives—a trifle too dramatically perhaps—upon the stage or in books.

In such cases, the adopted name often assumes important proportions that enable it to overshadow the full name; and the Number of Development virtually becomes a new Number of Destiny.

Take the case of Mark Twain. His vibratory Number of Destiny was 7, from the name Samuel Langhorne Clemens. His nom-de-plume vibrated to the number 8. The number 8 is a number of achievement, but it represents the scientist and the business man and not the author. It is interesting to note that Mark Twain spent his younger days under the influence of number 7, which is a mysterious number, indicating conservatism and lack of attainment. It was after his adoption of the name Mark Twain, with its vibratory number 8 that he achieved financial success, and most persons get the impression of achievement from the name Mark Twain.

The vibration of 7 governs the name Samuel L. Clemens, which was Mark Twain's first adopted name, and, therefore, it marked no real change in his career.

So here we see the significance of the adopted name, and its Number of Development. Starting with 7, a rather unaccountable number, with varied potentialities, Mark Twain adopted the name of Samuel L. Clemens, and made no progress. For years he plodded along, without achievement, handicapped by a number that hindered expression, yet gaining experiences that were to be of great value later on. When he finally came into his proper field of endeavor, he adopted the name Mark Twain, with its vibratory number (8) of material achievement, and so famous did his name become that he actually came under the vibratory influence of 8. Yet with it all, the vibratory number 7 held its place of importance. We must not forget the fact, also, that 22 was Mark Twain's Birth Number, and its signifies either phenomenal achievement or disaster. Coupled with the mystic number 7, 22 indicated real success and fame for Samuel Langhorne Clemens. Reducing to 4 the primary Birth Number produced a natural capacity for careful work.

The foregoing example has been given because it represents one of the most complex cases of Numerology. It illustrates how the names of adoption produce Numbers of Development that have a definite power over the periods in which they operate; yet it also shows the importance of the Number of Destiny in a case where the original name has long been discarded.

Thus we find that:

The adopted name produces a Number of Development which influences the individual to the extent that he uses it and lives up to it; but *it does not bring success or fame. It has no power to utterly change the life of the individual.*

A man cannot say: "I would like 5 as my

vibratory number," and proceed at once to adopt a name with that vibration, expecting to immediately assume all the characteristics of 5. The numbers of Numerology cast their influences, and those influences are deep-set. He who would bring a new vibratory influence into his life must first make himself worthy of that influence by a process of long and careful endeavor; and even then he may never achieve his desire.

We often see people who have pleasing manners, recognized ability, and flashes of genius, yet who are never successful. Their hopelessness of situation is usually because they lack some vital power toward progress, or because the qualities which they do possess are not deep-set or capable of proper functioning.

So it is with the name of adoption. If it serves merely as a tag of identification by which we may tell the person who possesses it, it will have a weak and useless vibratory number; but if it radiates the personality of the individual, and is developed and kept honest and straightforward, it will be a real source of power and a means of attainment.

There is an old expression: "I wouldn't have my name connected with that!" When a person speaks thus, he is admitting that *his name represents himself;* and that he realizes the importance of his name to him. The man who is careless of his name will ruin its potentiality, and may even go so far as to let his name gain evil and sinister powers that will make it a great force over which he has no control.

Some people have adopted new names because their old ones have come into disrepute, and have branded them as undesirable persons. Such is the power of the name; and it stands to reason that a new name of adoption, taken to replace a name that signifies badness, will be nothing more than a makeshift mask that will never be more than a mere attempt at camouflage.

When, however, a person has experienced a great change in life, and has entered upon a period of regeneration, that is sincere, a change of name becomes a different matter.

We have the Biblical accounts of Abram, who became Abraham; and Saul of Tarsus, whose name was changed to Paul. These were cases of real change of character; a new and vital influence in life which made the old name lose its significance.

One of the most interesting phases of Numerology is that which deals with the adoption, by a woman, of a married name. Here we have a case of an entire change of entire name; or rather, the assumption of an additional name.

This produces a new Number of Destiny, as well as a new Number of Development; and it is fitting that it should; for marriage, to a woman, means a change in career, and the assumption of new interests. With a man, marriage is an event; with a woman, it is the beginning of a new period of existence.

The full significance of this name, which assumes its full form as a matter of consequence, is discussed under the chapter on "The Number of Destiny." But the change also brings about the adoption of a new name, that is to come into general use. For example: A girl is named Charlotte Elizabeth Jones, and uses the name Charlotte Jones. Her Number of Development is derived from the total 57, which makes 12, and produces the vibratory number 3.

Upon marrying a man named Wilton, she adopts the name of Charlotte J. Wilton. This gives a total of 63 = 9; so 9 is her new Number of Development. The effect of the new vibration will, at first, be restricted to her new acquaintances; for the old ones will still remember her by her maiden name; but soon the influence of the new number will set in, and it may produce pronounced changes in characteristics.

Nowadays, some women retain their maiden names after marriage, especially when they are well known by their maiden names. Such a practice preserves the old Number of Development, although a new name of adoption may occasionally creep in, and have a slight influence. But it does not alter the new Number of Destiny.

The use of the title senior or junior, second, third, etc., after a name has no significance whatever. It means nothing more than Mister or Miss as a prefix to a name.

Each person must, therefore, study with much care his or her Number of Development, as determined by the name of adoption. The exact significance of such numbers is determined largely by the individual. In such well-known names as John D. Rockefeller, P. T. Barnum, etc., the Number of Development is of high significance.

The following summary will be of assistance:

(1) If the name is a natural contraction of the full name, development will be natural and steady.

(2) If the name is an affectation, or in the form of a nickname, it will be of less importance, unless it becomes widely known.

(3) An assumed name means nothing unless it is attended by achievement. Even then, it may only represent a superficial study of individual characteristics, unless the person acutally lives the life indicated by the new name.

(4) A married name, adopted by a woman, produces a new Number of Development which will immediately begin to be effective, with its new vibratory number.

(5) A normal change of existing names, as the

change from John W. Wallace to J. William Wallace, will also produce a new and natural Number of Development.

(6) The assumption of a stage name, or nom-de-plume, with a real purpose in mind, will sometimes bring about a new vibratory influence, if, as stated under paragraph 3, the person actually lives the life indicated by the new name.

The NUMBER OF DEVELOPMENT indicates the vibration that will influence people who hear about the individual or with whom the individual comes in brief contact. It also indicates the particular channel or means of progress along which the individual may develop the natural talents which he possesses. It is often advisable to supplant an inharmonious name of adoption with one that gives a better vibratory number; but a new Number of Development cannot overcome a deep-set, well-centered number that already exists; nor can it alter past circumstances; nor can it eradicate the Number of Destiny.

The Number of Development stands as a potential factor in future progress, and its success depends entirely upon the natural qualifications of the individual to make the most of it.

XVII. SUMMARIZING YOUR NUMEROLOGY

There are three simple steps in the summarizing of the Numerology of any person. The only difficulties that may arise are caused by complexities of modern nomenclature. Numerology itself is clear and understandable; but today there is a tendency toward ornate names.

The way to work out the significance of your vibratory numbers is to follow a regular course of procedure. The person with a comparatively simple name will then have no trouble whatever.

The three important steps are as follows:

(1) Find the Birth Number. (From the date of birth.)

(2) Find the Number of Destiny. (From the total name.)

(3) Find the Number of Development. (From the adopted name.)

Suppose that you find the Birth Number of a certain person to be 6. This would indicate that the person was born on a harmonious date, and would have tendencies to develop a dependable, evenly balanced character. That number would bear an important relationship to many natural traits, especially those pertaining to love and friendship. It would also account for certain likes, dislikes and peculiar instincts.

Assuming the Number of Destiny to be 1, we find there an important, progressive tendency that will be constant through life. It will not develop in early life, as will the Birth Number; and it may be overruled later on, after an adopted name has gained power; but it will always be a factor that will demand recognition. The number 1 will indicate strength of purpose, self-reliance, with possible distinction. Number 6 will provide stability to number 1, but there will always be a possible misunderstanding of desires caused by the action of 1 on 6.

As 6 will be the influence of early life, this means that early childhood should be tranquil and contented; then, as number 1 begins to take effect, there will be desire for progress, and at first self-discord with the passing of old illusions and cherished ideals. But as 1 progresses and assumes greater sway, the balancing influence of 6 will cause the beginning of more practical ambitions, and the result should be a rapid self-development.

Considering the Number of Development to be 7, and assuming that the adopted name is constantly used, so as to be commonly accepted, the result will not be good. Number 7 will first add depth to number 1, and will gradually bring a progressive tendency toward knowledge and intellectual attainments; but as the exaltation of number 7 develops, and it gains more importance, the presence of number 1 will be troublesome and annoying. There will be a desire for meditation and learning, which will be difficult to attain as it has been founded upon an earlier career which was entirely different. The choice of number 7 as a number of development is apt to prove to be a bad one.

Note one thing in favor, however. That is the existence of 6 as a Birth Number. There should be sufficient power in 6 to aid in the development of 7; but the effect of 7, the Number of Development, upon 6, the Birth Number, will be practically nil, as the Number of Destiny will serve as a sort of buffer between them.

The result will be a conflict; a hard struggle in the development of number 7, greatly hindered by number 1, but partially aided by the ever present influence of number 6.

There is a rule that should be emphasized here, at the conclusion of the brief summary:

The effect of an existing number is stronger upon a new influence that comes into being than is the new influence upon the old.

Furthermore:

The presence of an intermediate number pre-

*vents the influence of a new number upon those
which have existed before.*

Thus, while the Number of Destiny first influences the Birth Number, the logical result will
be the rise of the Number of Destiny *influenced
by* the Birth Number.

Then, while the Number of Development will
first influence the Number of Destiny, the logical
result will be the rise of the Number of Development *influenced by* the Number of Destiny.

But the Number of Development will not influence the Birth Number to any degree, for the
most active period of the Birth Number is past.
The Number of Development, however, will still
be partially *influenced by* the Birth Number.

Suppose that a new name is legitimately adopted; either through reasonable circumstances, or
because the person is a woman who becomes married. Let us suppose that the new name reduces
to 2, giving 2 as the new Number of Development.

We must then consider three things:

(1) The harmonizing, or conflicts of numbers
7 and 2, during the period in which the new vibratory influence is replacing the old, and also any
permanent effect that the discarded Number of
Development may have on the new one.

(2) The influence of the Number of Destiny,
upon the new Number of Development.

(3) The influence of the Birth Number upon the new Number of Development.

Under the first heading we find that 2 is well understood, but not strengthening to 7. This means that the new vibratory influence will make no pronounced change in the person's development, but it will be readily accepted, and will soon begin to take effect, with no harmful consequences.

As number 2 becomes the important Number of Development, the influence of 7 upon 2 is of important consideration. We learn that 7 gives vision, but not action to number 2. Hence, as far as the Numbers of Development are concerned, affairs will be bettered, but to no remarkable degree.

The number 1, which is the Number of Destiny, will add some of the needed strength to the new Number of Development, 2, but it may cause trouble and conflict. However, as 1 was not harmonious with 7, the old Number of Development, this change should also be for the better.

The number 6, which is the Birth Number, will help 2, but will not give impetus. It will not be as strong a factor in the development of 2 as it was with number 7, the old Number of Development, and the influence of 6 will be somewhat lost.

We can, therefore, summarize and outline the Numerological influences in this person's life, and

give a résumé of the indications which should be
most effective.

The early childhood should be tranquil and
contented, fond of idealism, and placidly happy.
As the person grows older, there will be an influx
of youthful ambitions, which will shatter old
ideals and will bring ambitions and desires that
will prove impracticable for a time.

Then, as this new course of action begins to
take hold, there will come a yearning for the deeper things of life, and an inclination toward knowledge that will cause regret because of wasted effort and shallowness of ambitions. There will
always be some conflict while 7, the first Number
of Development, is in sway, influenced by the progressive 1. The old ideals of childhood will be
reconsidered, and will prove of some assistance;
but harmony will be difficult of attainment.

The beginning of 2, as a new Number of Development, will mean a gradual change, without
any immediate results. But in the course of time
this person will gain greater vision and some contentment. He or she will become thoughtful and
fair-minded, but will still be indecisive and changeable. The presence of Number 1 as the Number
of Destiny will cause spasmodic yearnings for
progress, and will lead to sudden bursts of action;
but those periods will not always be advantageous. The very actions that will bring success at

one time will result in failure at another. There will be a realization that constant effort should be adopted; but procrastination and hesitation will be hindering influences. At the same time, the childhood ideals evidenced by number 6 will remain; but they will be less evident than they were before.

It must be remembered that the Number of Development gains greater importance with the wideness of acquaintanceship and prestige of the individual. If the person who has these vibratory influences is, through circumstances, restricted to a very small field of action, he or she will profit more by the Number of Destiny, 1, and may achieve much success and progress in a small way. But should the person enter into widespread enterprises, his or her importance will probably be lost, and the person will be overwhelmed by the greater activities and achievements of others.

The real field for development for such a person lies, therefore, in a small community. His or her education should progress better in a small institution. If such a person can be contented in these surroundings, the chances for high development will be much more likely; for many people who achieve fame in a small way are often called to greater duties which they could not have performed at an earlier period.

As another example consider a person whose

Birth Number is 3; whose Number of Destiny is 5; and whose Number of Achievement is 9.

Such a person will be happy, active and versatile in childhood, and should enter upon an adventurous and exciting career, choosing those things that offer novelty. The influence of 3 should be helpful during this period, which should be instructive, though not progressive. As the number 9 comes into being as the Number of Development, it will prove helpful to number 5; but it will not be a steadying influence, unless it takes a firm hold. Should this person enter into widespread undertakings, and create a broad field of acquaintanceship, the number 9 would be exalted, and would show the way to great achievement; for it would be helped and urged onward by both numbers 3 and 5.

If a change of the Number of Development should bring in the number 4, there would at first be a favorable action of 4 upon 9, which would be reciprocated by 9 upon 4, when the latter number should begin to take its greatest effect. In the same way, 3 would be harmonious with 4, and the individual should make great progress along specific lines requiring great exactitude. The only note of conflict would be the influence of 5 upon 4. There would still be the periodic moments of restlessness and longing for change of scene that might occasionally be injurious to the real work and desires of the individual.

It will be observed that while every person has a number of important vibratory influences in his or her life, it is not difficult to trace the particular importance of each one during a certain period. In fact, it is much easier to analyze a particular case than it is to deal in generalities. This statement means that in an individual case, one can tell almost the exact age of the person when a change of name or the development of a name took effect. The best way to consider future indications is to study past ones, and see how they are operating at present. Then the future is not hard to analyze.

Vibratory numbers have peculiar tendency to display themselves in sudden, instinctive ways. Thus a person whose Birth Number is 7 may have an occasional desire for meditation that he has never been able to explain before he studied Numerology. If the same person has come under the active sway of certain other vibratory numbers, the presence of 7 may take an opposite course, and produce an instinctive dread of loneliness and a fear of gloomy surroundings.

When we study that 1 is the symbol of Unity; 2 the symbol of Diplomacy; 3 of Versatility and so on, and go deeper into the characteristics of each number, we must realize that each trait has

retroactive as well as active possibilities, and may
sometimes lead in the wrong direction. All bad
indications are unfortunate developments of good
ones.

The foregoing summary deals with the fundamental importance of numbers. The Birth Number, the Number of Destiny, and the Number of
Development—or the Numbers of Development,
form the great structure upon which indications
are built.

The other numbers which were mentioned in
the preceding chapter are like fine threads woven
into a solid fabric. They add color or somber-
ness, and give points of individuality; although
they may never fade, they add no strength or
durability to the fabric itself.

In infancy, the Name Number often finds a
temporary exaltation, and it can be considered in
the moods and actions of children who are just
coming to the age where they learn to walk and
talk.

The active name evidences certain traits in
childhood and maturity. If we know two men
with the same first name, we think of them at the
same time, and subconsciously find slight points in
common although their great characteristics may
be entirely different. There is a superficial tendency about the active name that is a slight bond
between people who have it; and if you think of

people you know who have the same active name as you, you will note a peculiar tone of sympathy and understanding that is more often evident than lacking.

The passive name is of very little importance as a rule. It sometimes evidences itself, but its power is very, very faint in most cases. It is only when it has a hereditary significance that it is likely to become even a possible factor.

The hereditary name should be carefully considered, for if it is a true representation of family traits, it may be of considerable importance. It seems to persist through all stages of life; but much of its real significance comes outside the sphere of Numerology.

If you take the numbers from 1 to 9 inclusive, and arrange them in different ways, using seven numbers in each arrangement, you will soon realize that a vast multitude of combinations are possible. This fact harmonizes Numerology with life. It is seldom that we see two people whose characteristics are extremely close in every detail; and it is also very seldom that we find two people whose numbers correspond exactly, especially when we include the exact periods of life at which each particular number may experience its greatest significance.

The chances of two people being identical in all their shades of characteristics are almost infinitesimal; and in the same way, the chances of two persons having Numerologies which are precisely the same are also very remote. Thus Numerology is in accord with life and does not conflict with recognized conditions.

There is an apt quotation from Fitzgerald's Rubaiyat of Omar Khayyam, which reads:

"And fear not lest Existence closing your
"Account, should lose, or know the type no more."

This carries the very thought of Numerology. It leaves room for differences in individuals, and offers great possibilities for variations of development; but, at the same time, like Existence, it knows and illustrates types which have survived for ages, and which will continue to appear in the centuries that lie ahead.

NUMEROLOGICAL CHART—Periods of Life

Numbers	Infancy	Childhood	Maturity	Later Life	Indications
BIRTH					Deep set characteristics Love Friendship
Name					
DESTINY					Attained Characteristics dependent upon Development
Active					
Passive					
Hereditary					
DEVELOPMENT					Traits gained through life in connection with the importance of the name.

In this chart the solid lines point to the indications and represent the Numerological factors that are of great importance. The dotted lines are of minor significance.

The increasing or decreasing thickness of each line indicates its comparative importance during the specific period.

In cases where the full name is the adopted name, the Numbers of Destiny and Development will coincide.

XVIII. The NUMBERS OF THE DAYS

Every day has its vibratory number.

This is determined by simply adding the number of the month, the day, and the year.

The Declaration of Independence was signed on July 4, 1776. The figures 7, 4, 1, 7, 7, 6 total 32, and give the vibration 5. That is a number of adventure, uncertainty, and possible failure. It was significant of the troubled times, and the hazardous undertaking which was involved.

The day of the great Armistice was November 11, 1918. The figures 1, 1, 1, 1, 1, 9, 1, 8 total 23, and give the number 5. The Armistice also represented an adventurous project; the beginning of an era of uncertainty and peculiar conditions. The predomination of the number 1, however, which occurs six times, is really significant; for it indicates a strength of certainty amid a cloud of restlessness.

The birthday of Abraham Lincoln occurred on February 12, 1809. Here, from 2-12-1809 comes the total of 23, which reduces to 5. The stalwart, powerful character of Lincoln was found in his Number of Destiny, which, coming from a total of 45, reduced to 9, the symbol of universal power, integrity, high development and great leadership; yet the ever present influence of the uncertain number 5 brought him into leadership during a period of adventure and uncertainty, which culminated in his untimely death, just after the realization of his hopes.

The vibratory number of each day is an important matter, and something is to be gained by considering the number of a day before undertaking any great enterprise.

If a person finds that number 3, for example, is the number of greatest vibration in his or her life, days that possess that number will be particularly productive. The number of the day should be closely compared with the Birth Number. If the two are identical, it is a good sign; if they are harmonious, conditions are also good; if the numbers have little in common, the day is doubtful; and it is advisable to be cautious on a day which has a number that is inharmonious with the Birth Number.

As every day vibrates a certain primary number, each day also has its own field of endeavor. A day with the vibration of 8 is good for business enterprises; financial failures are apt to occur on a day which has the uncertain vibration of 5.

Columbus set out on his voyage of discovery on the third of August, 1492. The numbers 8-3-

1492 produce the sum of 27, which reduces to 9, the greatest number for achievement.

The Titanic set sail on April 14, 1912. The number of 4-14-1912 is 22, a mystic, dangerous number that in this case signified disaster.

Countless other examples could be given, illustrating how days of certain vibration have been productive of good fortune or indicative of bad results. In great battles, fought on certain days, the vibratory number of one side has been in harmony with the day, and success has resulted for that army; it is also possible to trace instances where the tide has turned with the changing of the vibratory number, on the coming of the new day.

So first of all, the day itself should be considered, and its vibration taken upon its own merits. That will give the general trend of the day. If a question of individual enterprise is involved, compare the Birth Number with the number of the particular day. The Number of Destiny, or a strong Number of Development, should also be compared if an issue is at stake; but under most circumstances, the Number of Birth is the chief one to be considered in this connection.

Remember that a day which is not in harmony with one person's vibratory number may be just the proper day for another person. This is a subject that demands careful attention, for it may often indicate the result of a contest.

The day of the week has a minor significance.
Sunday vibrates to 1 and 8; Monday to 2 and 9;
Tuesday to 3; Wednesday to 4; Thursday to 5;
Friday to 6, and Saturday to 7. These vibrations
are of small significance unless one of them happens to be the same as the numerical vibration of
the day. In that case, it will strengthen the vibratory number of the day. In the opposite way, if
the day of the week has a vibratory number that
is decidedly inharmonious with the vibratory number of the day, the power of the day will be
slightly weakened.

Sunday and Monday are always uncertain quantities, for sometimes both their numbers function,
and at others, one number predominates and rules
completely. The familiar "Blue Monday" is
usually a day when number 2, with opposite, conflicting interests, is present instead of 9.

When 9 is in power, Monday should be a day
of achievement, the beginning of a successful
week.

In the case of Sunday, numbers 1 and 8 have
much in common, and produce great possibilities
of progress.

But the day of the week and its vibratory number should always be subordinated, and should be
considered merely as an afterthought. The number of the day is the vital subject, and it has acted

in the past, and will act in the future, very powerfully in the affairs of the human race.

The numbers of the days and importance of their vibratory influences are, briefly:

1.—A day of progress, purpose and uniformity.

2.—A day of indecision, but also of quietness and balance.

3.—A day of action, quick developments and activity.

4.—A day of routine and labor.

5.—A day of excitement and surprises.

6.—A day of completion and harmonious conditions.

7.—A day of gloom and deep thought.

8.—A day of enterprise and establishment.

9.—A day of power and achievement.

The significance of each day, as just given, applies to the affairs of ordinary life. The day itself does not introduce a vibratory influence into the individual; each person must apply his own vibration to that of the day.

When a person is born upon a certain day, circumstances are entirely different. As he or she then becomes an active, individual factor in worldly affairs the natural result is the absorption of the influences existing on that day; and hence the Birth Number of the person is established.

The subsequent birthday anniversaries of a person are of no consequence except when they possess exactly the same vibration as did the date of birth. Then the birthday anniversary should be a most active one.

The same is true of wedding anniversaries and anniversaries of great events.

The real culmination of the vibratory influence of any period comes in the number obtained from the particular figures found in the day, month and year.

As has been mentioned, the day itself has a slight individual vibration according to whether it is Monday, Tuesday, Wednesday, etc.

In the same way, each month may be given a special vibratory influence as 1 for January, 2 for February, and so on, October vibrating to 1, November to 2, and December to 3.

Each year may be given a vibratory influence carrying throughout the year. It is interesting to observe that Peary discovered the North Pole in the year 1909, which vibrates to the number 1, significant of constant endeavor; and that the World War came to an end in 1918 through the result of a driving powerful form of action, also signified by 1.

But all these observations are of lesser importance, just as are attempts to give vibratory influences to hours and minutes. The day is the real unit of human activity; and through the date, month and year we determine the day itself.

Four days show their significance in the career of Napoleon. He was born on August 15, 1769, the number of which is 1, the symbol of progress. He was made Emperor of France December 2, 1804, (12-2-1804), and crowned King of Italy May 26, 1805 (5-26-1805). Each of these days has 9 as its number; and 9 is the number of high achievement. Napoleon died May 5, 1821 (5-5-1821), the number of the day being 4, which stands for obscurity.

XIX. NUMBERS IN EVERY-DAY LIFE

Numbers apply to all affairs of mankind. Places, localities, countries, animals and objects all respond to vibrations, according to Numerology.

The number of the battleship "Maine" was sixteen, which indicates evil results and disaster. In the old symbolism, it stood for a fallen castle. The number of the "Titanic" was 18, signifying darkness, gloom, and unhappiness. The famous cruiser "Emden" of the German navy totalled 23, which comes above the range of the secondary numbers; but its primary number was 5, signifying travel, adventure, uncontrolled activity and possible misfortune.

The total of the letters in England are 26, giving the vibratory number of 8, which indicates high development, completion, widespread activity and successful power.

France, with a total of 23, reduces to the vibratory number 5, indicating adventure, sweeping power, spasmodic brilliancy, and great upheaval or change.

Italy vibrates to the number 1, and this explains

the response of that country to the policy of Mussolini, with his desire for a unified, aggressive and ambitious nation.

The total of the letters in The United States of America is 90, which reduces to 9, the number of magnetism and universal influence, power and regeneration.

Cities, too, have their vibrations. New York, and Boston, each with the number 1, have risen to be great cities because of their self-reliance, distinction, and ability to expand during the early days of development.

Chicago, with its vibratory number 6, is a city of attainment. The number 6 does not have the singleness of purpose found in 1, but it indicates solid expansion under favorable conditions.

London vibrates to the number 4, and indicates slow but constant growth, with endurance. The city is not characterized by the sudden progress seen in so many American cities.

Philadelphia has the vibratory number 8, which indicates prosperity and material success. Despite its closeness to New York, Philadelphia has an individuality all its own, and represents an independent type. At one time, Philadelphia was the largest city in the United States, and also the capital. The loss of those two distinctions is typical of number 8, which signifies completion with a lessening of aggressive effort.

Paris has the total of 15, the number of willfulness, which signifies riot and lawlessness. Those elements have been notoriously rampant in Paris; yet the primary vibration—6—has produced a city of brilliancy and artistic development.

The names of suburbs, apartment houses, street addreses, etc., all have their significance. Where street numbers are considered, the number itself is of major importance, and it must be reduced to a vibratory number. The same is true of telephone numbers.

Numbers, themselves, produce more definite results than do letters, because they do not require translation. In considering street addresses, it is well to sum up the numbers of the letters and find their significance when added to the house number. Suffixed words, as street, avenue, etc., should be included.

But in counting up telephone numbers, the name of the exchange should not be included, as it is arbitrary, and has no exact locality.

The author has a friend whose phone number is 8267. The figures add up to 23, and produce the vibration of 5. That telephone is notorious for its percentage of wrong calls, and is typical of the number 5.

Coming to animals, we may find that they are subject, in a minor degree, to vibrations of primary numbers. Kipling tells of "the cat that walked by itself"; and the letters C-A-T add up to 7, giving the vibratory number 7, a symbol of loneliness.   Cats, as a rule, like their own company best, and they become friendly only when they feel that it is to their advantage.

The dashing, adventurous spirit of the dog is found in the number 5; the hidden intelligence of the horse, ever present yet seldom revealed, is typical of number 7, produced from 25, the total of H-O-R-S-E; while the cow, peaceful by nature, is indicated by number 6.

When a name is bestowed upon a dog, or a horse, the animal frequently exhibits traits that are indicated by the Numerology of that name.

What is the significance of all these observations?   Just this: a careful consideration of all numerical vibrations will enable us to choose the conditions which are most harmonious to our welfare, and to our own vibratory numbers; and also help us to avoid conditions that are injurious.

Numerology is not a form of superstition; for it is founded upon definitely established principles, based on ancient learning.   People who have studied Numerology do not talk of lucky numbers, chosen at random, and feared or liked because of hearsay.   Instead, they seek to analyze, and to compare the results that actually occur in their own experience.   In this way they find which numbers are harmonious to themselves, and are best adapted to their interests.

There is no hard and fast rule governing any phase of human life. Numbers are immutable, when they deal with time, space, and distances; but when they are interpreted to meet human needs, they become flexible, and are often elusive and not properly understood.

The modern science of Numerology is young, and must be learned slowly, just as simple arithmetic must be mastered before one can proceed to an understanding of higher mathematics.

The person who analyzes all vibrations, and tries to interpret their meanings will learn much practical knowledge, and will achieve real results. He will also meet with failure and will make mistakes; but until he can really say that he has mastered all the intricacies of Numerology, he must, in fairness, attribute the errors to his own misinterpretation, rather than to the laws of the science of Numerology.

XX. FACTS REVEALED BY NUMBERS

Numerology deals with the significance of names and dates according to numbers. It has as its foundation, the Kabbala of Numbers, and there is enough interesting material in the history of numbers to fill a great volume. In fact, the student of numbers becomes more and more convinced, as he pursues his reading, that numbers have a real influence in the affairs of the world, and that many events of importance can be classified mathematically, just as the distances to the stars and the orbits of the heavenly bodies are tabulated through the application of mathematical principles.

The present chapter is intended to reveal certain little known facts that are so remarkable that they seem to be more than mere coincidence.

In the discovery of certain future events, years alone are considered; and by means of a vertical tabulation, results are obtained. While these events are not usually applicable to individuals, there are notable instances in which they have indicated the future of important personages very clearly. For example:

Queen Victoria was born in.....1819
Adding the figures—

I
8
I
9
———

The Year Victoria became queen 1838

The year obtained by this addition may be called the Year of Attainment. This does not mean that it will be a year of success; it may be a year of calamity; but it will represent a year of greatest importance.

Generally the Year of Attainment is determined by adding the figures of an important previous year. Sometimes a prediction is made in a certain year, and that year forms the basis for the tabulation.

It is only in a comparatively few cases that a vertical tabulation will bring a tangible result; but the strange thing about it is that when one result is obtained, it frequently marks the beginning of a series of remarkable numerical predictions.

For example:

In the year 1828, a woman named Katherine Speesman went to Berlin, and in the year 1829 had gained a reputation as a seeress. She was asked by Prince William, brother of the Prussian King

Frederick William, to predict his future political achievements.

By a vertical tabulation, she produced the result:

$$1829$$
$$1$$
$$8$$
$$2$$
$$9$$
$$\overline{}$$
$$1849$$

That year was predicted as a time when order would be firmly established by the Prince. In 1849, he suppressed a revolutionary uprising.

The Prince, so the story goes, asked if he would ever become ruler of a unified Germany.

The tabulation was continued:

Year of suppressed rebellion.....1849
$$1$$
$$8$$
$$4$$
$$9$$
$$\overline{}$$

Foundation of the German Empire..1871..

The next logical question was how long would Prince William rule over his established Empire. It was answered thus:

Foundation of the German Empire.... 1871

$$\begin{array}{r} 1 \\ 8 \\ 7 \\ 1 \\ \hline \end{array}$$

Death of the Emperor William...... 1888

That brought up the question: How long would the Empire survive. The vertical numeration showed:

Death of the Emperor William...... 1888

$$\begin{array}{r} 1 \\ 8 \\ 8 \\ 8 \\ \hline \end{array}$$

Last complete year of the Empire.... 1913

It is interesting to note that this prediction was recalled in the year 1912. The setting of 1913 as the last year of the German Empire was significant; because the disintegration of the Empire commenced the following year, with the seizure of German colonies; and although the Empire did not finally collapse until 1918, the year 1913 was the year of its greatest territorial expansion, and the decline then set in.

An interesting vertical tabulation is found in the history of the French Revolution:

Robespierre lost power in..........1794
$$1, 7, 9, 4 = \quad 21$$

The overthrow of Napoleon.........1815
$$1, 8, 1, 5 = \quad 15$$

The fall of Charles X.............1830
$$1, 8, 3, 0 = \quad 12$$

Death of the Duke of Orleans, Heir-
apparent to the French throne.....1842

There is a similar table that applies to the rule
of English kings, commencing with the accession
of George I.

George I. began to rule in..........1714
$$1, 7, 1, 4 = \quad 13$$

Accession of George II.............1727
$$1, 7, 2, 7 = \quad 17$$

Year of Stuart Rebellion...........1744
$$1, 7, 4, 4 = \quad 16$$

George III ascended throne.........1760

The figures do not continue to the accession of
George IV. because the reign of George III. did
not come to a natural conclusion, George IV. act-
ing as Prince Regent from 1811 to 1820.

The number 36 possesses peculiar properties in

American history, commencing with the Revolution, and the signing of the Declaration of Independence in 1776

Add   36
_____

Beginning of War with England. .1812

Add   36
_____

End of the Mexican War.......1848

The Mexican War began in......1846

1, 8, 4, 6 =   19
_____

End of Civil War.............1865

The Mexican War began in......1846

Add 72 (twice 36)   72
_____

End of the Great War.........1918

First complete year of the Civil War. .1862

Add 36   36
_____

Year of Spanish-American War.......1898

Numerical additions of vertical numbers show:

Inauguration of United States Government 1789

1

7

8

9
_____

End of second war with England........1814

The loss of the ship "Philadelphia," the American failure in the attack on the Barbary Powers, occurred in ....,........1803

$$1$$
$$8$$
$$0$$
$$\underline{3}$$

The year Decatur defeated the Barbary Powers 1815

*   *   *   *   *   *

The most remarkable of all progressions in American history is that of the presidents.

William Henry Harrison was elected in 1840, and he died in office. Nine years later, Zachary Taylor died in office. Since that time, *every president elected in a year divisible by twenty, has died in office,* forming an unbroken chain beginning with Harrison; and *every fourth president following Taylor has died in office.* The two chains, or orders of progression have been identical, thus:

Elected in 1840   Harrison
                   Taylor
Elected in 1860   Lincoln
           Fourth President after Taylor
Elected in 1880   Garfield
           Fourth President after Lincoln.

Elected in 1900   McKinley
          Fourth President after Garfield.*
Elected in 1920   Harding
          Fourth President after McKinley.

The most remarkable of all cases of numerical prediction, and one that is based upon an uncanny combination of vertical additions are the tables of Louis Philippe, last King of France, and Napoleon III., last Emperor of France.

Louis Philippe ascended the throne in.... 1830
He was born in 1773, the figures totaling   18
                                            ____

Date of his fall..................... 1848
Again: He ascended the throne in..... 1830
His wife was born in 1782, a total of....   18
                                            ____

Date of the fall of Louis............. 1848
Furthermore: He ascended the throne in 1830
He was married in 1809, a total of......   18
                                            ____

Date of his fall...................... 1848

When Napoleon III. ascended the throne, he should have profited by the example of Louis Philippe; for unwittingly he placed himself at the

* McKinley was the fourth man to hold the office of President after Garfield. Cleveland was the twenty-second and the twenty-fourth President, but is, of course, counted as one man.

mercy of a table of numbers which produced exactly the same result!

Napoleon III. ascended the throne in. . . . 1853
He was born in 1808, the figures totaling   17
_____

He was deposed in. 1870
Again: He became Emperor in. 1853
His wife (Eugenie) was born in 1826. . . .   17
_____

Fall of Napoleon III. 1870
Furthermore: Napoleon III. ascended the
      throne in 1853
He was married in 1853, a total of.   17
_____

He was deposed in. 1870

This singular coincidence of numbers has been
known for thirty or forty years; but it was recalled when the two pretenders, one the lineal
successor of Louis Philippe, and the other the
successor of Napoleon III., died a few days apart,
in the year 1926.

Such are the results of vertical tabulations and
periodic intervals of years. Their exact significance is doubtful; but they form an interesting
phase of Numerology. Look for them in the
lives of different people, and remarkable results
will frequently occur. In your own life, great
events may occur in periods; and the year of one

noteworthy event, added in vertical form, may lead to a valuable prediction.

A most remarkable coincidence of numbers, and their relations to human affairs throughout the years is found in the careers of two modern masters of mystery.

In the latter part of the nineteenth century, one of the most mysterious and remarkable men then alive was the celebrated magician, Herrmann the Great, whose name was Alexander Herrmann, or Alexandre Herrmann.

Herrmann was born in the year 1844. Each of his names, Alexander and Herrmann, carry the vibratory influence of 5, a double symbol of desire for travel and adventure. The vibratory number of his name was 1, significant of achievement and progress along a certain distinctive line of work.

In 1896, while still at the height of his career, and while he was touring the country, Herrmann was stricken suddenly, and died at the age of 52.

In 1874, thirty years after the birth of Herrmann, another great mystifier was born; a man who was to gain great fame during the twentieth century. That man was Harry Houdini, both of whose names responded to the same vibration of Herrmann's, namely 5, and with the same total vibration of 1.

It is a notable fact that two men with identical

influences should both achieve widespread success in the same field of endeavor; but it is still more remarkable to consider that in 1926, Houdini, while touring the country, and at the height of his career, was also stricken and died at exactly the age of Herrmann, 52.   Thus the careers of these two great mystifiers showed a remarkable Numerological correspondence.   It might be mentioned also that 52 reduces to 7, the great number of mystery.

Here are some further tabulations from French history.

Napoleon I. was born in   1769
Add the figures 1, 7, 6, 9   1792

In the year 1792, Napoleon went to Paris and was commissioned a captain.   Now, two events follow.   Add 23 (the figures in 1769), once more, and they give 1815—the year of Napoleon's overthrow.

Or: Continuing from   1792
Add the figures, 1, 7, 9, 2   1811
Birth of the King of Rome 1811
Add the figures 1, 8, 1, 1,   1822

The year 1811 presaged a Napoleonic dynasty, but the dawn of 1822 spelled oblivion, for Napoleon died in the spring of 1821.

Another tabulation begins with the year of the death of Louis XV., in 1774.

Louis XVI. ascended the throne........1774

     1
     7
     7
     4
     ——

Death of Louis XVI.................1793

The eldest son of Louis XVI. died in....1789

     1
     7
     8
     9
     ——

Ascension of Louis XVIII.............1814

Now although Louis XVIII. ascended the throne in 1814, he was driven out by the return of Napoleon from Elba. The year following he returned to make his power secure, and, beginning with this latter date, the table corresponds with the Revolutionary table of France, thus:

Louis XVIII established..............1815

     1
     8
     1
     5
     ——

Fall of Charles X...................1830

Adding the figures of 1830............ 12
                                      ——

Death of Duke of Orleans...........1842

English history has shown us a remarkable chain of vertical tabulations, that began with the important year of 1830, and resumed operation after the broken chain of the house of Hanover, with its four Georges. All the important events given in the following list are found by adding the figures of each date to the date itself to determine the next date, as 1830 plus 1, 8, 3, 0 = 1842.

> William IV. ascended the throne in......1830
> Disaster in the invasion of Afghanistan..1842
> Great Indian Mutiny.................1857
> Second Afghan War.................1878
> Termination of the Boer War..........1902
> Outbreak of the European War........1914

This progression is unbroken up to 1914. Should it continue, as many other progressions have done, it would point to important events to Great Britain in the years 1929, 1950, and 1965. It should be observed, however, that this chain is unique in that it has been linked by events which were disastrous in many ways. The invasions of Afghanistan were beset with danger and misfortune, in over-proportion to the gain. The Indian mutiny was also disastrous, and the Boer war was beset with difficulties. The great war in Europe also brought trying times to England. Such military successes as the Crimean War fall outside the chain, which seems to be an undesirable one. So no one will regret the ending of the progression, for its termination should be a fortunate occurrence.

Reference has been made to Queen Victoria, who was born in 1819 and who ascended the throne in 1838. It is interesting to compare the tabulation taken from the year of Woodrow Wilson's birth, 1856. We have 1876 and 1898 as two years of attainment, with no indication of special events; but the year of Wilson's death falls upon the next year of attainment: for 1898, plus the figures 1, 8, 9, 8, gives 1924.

XXI. THE APPLICATION OF NUMER-
OLOGY

The person who has read the previous chapters has, by this time, a good understanding of the fundamental principles of the science. All through this book, the purpose has been to give suggestions for application whenever a definite statement has been made. But it is quite important and essential that the student should not gain a false impression of the true meaning of Numerology, or lay too much emphasis upon any particular phase of the subject.

No one should look upon Numerology as the one great key to success; an infallible oracle that should be consulted frequently and trusted implicitly. Such procedure would defeat the very aim of the science, which seeks to further human understanding and bring enlightenment; not to stifle individuality.

Much has been written in favor of such ancient subjects as Astrology and Palmistry; but, unfortunately, they have been practiced so steadily during the past centuries that superstition has crept about them, and it is very difficult to separate the chaff from the wheat. Numerology is as old as the hills; but for many years it has lain in obscurity, and has been kept alive only through the efforts of true scholars, who have not been guided by ulterior purposes. Now that it is coming into its own once more, it has a clean slate, and possesses great possibilities for the future. None of the self-styled mystic seers, astrologists, and palmists who have been constantly looking for easy money have, as yet, invaded the clear field of Numerology. There are no "numerologists" who are seeking dupes; instead, there are quite a few sincere students who are endeavoring to test the possibilities of Numerology, and who are just as anxious to dispel fallacies as they are to establish facts.

The person who becomes interested in Numerology should, therefore, rely upon his own judgment. It is not necessary for him to delve into intricate mathematical calculations in order to apply the principles of Numerology. Instead, he should avoid complications, and should content himself with experiments conducted along a recognized and established line, such as the system of numeration outlined in this book.

No person should feel that he is misplaced in life simply because his Numerology does not suit his desires. The characteristics of the individual may be likened to a long chain, composed of many different links. We all know the truth of the old saying that "a chain is as strong as its weakest link." The material of which this imaginary or mental chain is made is always close at hand, and it is within the power of every person to weld new links to replace or strengthen weak ones. Numerology simply indicates where those faulty links lie; it does not state that they can never be mended. Hence it gives information which is of practical value, and, in some cases, shows the way to higher and better development.

There are no such things as "lucky days,'" "lucky colors," "lucky stones," and the like, in Numerology. The science is not built upon superstition, and superstition has not been built upon it. The future possibilities of Numerology depend upon preventing any foolish notions to creep into its indications.

Thus if a person discovers that a certain day of a certain year is under a vibratory influence which conflicts with his own, he should not adopt the foolish course of trying to avoid all enterprises on that particular day. Such a plan of action would be in utter disagreement with the real purposes of Numerology. The proper course would be to make unusual effort during the period or day, and thus prove that real concentration and desire to succeed are the greatest powers in life.

Many people attribute great importance to Numerology because through it they learn of peculiarities which they possess, but have never really understood. If they stop there, they have learned nothing of real value; nothing more than something their friends have always been able to tell them, but have refrained from doing. Once a person has really identified himself with the influences of certain vibratory nombers, he should make it a great purpose to apply that new-found knowledge in practical, sensible ways.

Numerology is just as constant as mathematics; but it is much more difficult to interpret numbers than it is to multiply them. Take two large numbers, and try to multiply them mentally. There will probably be an error in calculation, but you should be able to approximate the result. The interpretation of Numerological indications presents a similar problem. The true significance can be approximated but not always identified.

The first step in the application of Numerology is to discover the vibratory influences which exist in the individual. Having done this, the next step is to try to strengthen all weaknesses, and to modify any characteristics which are likely to be over-developed, to the disadvantage of others. Then one may study the minor influences which surround him, and should endeavor to better them, or try to adapt himself to them.

For example: suppose a person has a friend of

many years' standing, but with whom he has had certain disagreements. Through Numerology, he finds that there is a conflict of vibratory influences between him and the friend. What should he do? Forget his friend and seek a new one? Certainly not. On the contrary, he should study the points wherein the vibratory influences conflict, and he will probably find that he can come to a plan of action that will lead to permanent understanding. If a study of Numerology can give indications of this sort, that lead to self-realization, it matters not what its reliability may be; it will have served a useful, helpful purpose and will have aided human happiness.

Let us refer to a specific case. A man and a woman were happily married, but their matrimonial bliss was disturbed by quarrels that occurred with too great a frequency. One never seemed to be able to appreciate the other's viewpoint. Through Numerology, the husband learned that he possessed the vibratory influence of Number 1, while his wife had the Birth Number of 7. This immediately brought about a better understanding, for the husband realized that he had a tendency to follow his own interests with disregard for those of other people; and more than that, he recognized the fact that he did not follow such a course with any intent of meanness. But such a procedure could never be fully accepted by the meditative person influenced by number 7. It also enabled him to appreciate how easily loneliness and apprehension could destroy his wife's happiness. So he gained valuable advice which he probably would not have accepted if some person had given it to him. With a fresh point of view, he was enabled to work for a more mutual understanding, and to avoid actions that would cause unhappiness.

As another instance, two business associates were active and well-established, yet one occasionally semed to tire of the work much to the annoyance of his partner. Finally the partner learned that while he had the vibratory influence of 8 as his Number of Development, his associate came under the sway of number 5. This discovery enabled him to make allowances for his associate's restlessness, for he quickly realized that to number 5, the great spice of life is certainly variety. In his future plans, therefore, the man of number 8 saw to it that his associate did all business that required travel, or involved novel developments.

Many further examples could be cited; but the reader should apply them for himself. It is not difficult to understand why two people do not get along together, after summing up their vibratory influences, and finding them inharmonious. But the great thing to remember is that Numerology can always pave the way to a better understanding and can often supply the necessary spark that produces the flame of achievement.

No one should change his name because he or she is not satisfied with the present vibratory influence. Such a procedure would be artificial in nature, and would have no good effect; in fact, it would be injurious, for it would smother all development of the existing vibratory influence, and would create a false mental condition.

A modification of a name, such as the omission, or the utilization of a middle initial is sometimes a helpful procedure, especially if it serves a useful purpose other than the effort to form a new number of development. For instance John Jones, with a total of 42 and the vibratory influence of 6, is often confused with a man of the same name, much to the disadvantage of both. So he utilizes his middle initial C., making his name John C. Jones, producing a total of 44 and a vibratory influence of 8, which he may feel is more in harmony with the conditions that surround him. As people will immediately take advantage of the change in order to serve their own convenience, there is little doubt that the new Number of Development will gradually begin to take effect.

The utilization of a complete middle name, or the shift from a first name to another is justifiable if the new name carries dignity and balance.

A most interesting example of name changing

is found in the life story of the late President
Wilson. It is said that he studied the effective-
ness of names, not from the standpoint of Numerology, but with the idea that a well-balanced and
even-sounding name was more desirable than one
that seemed more prosaic. Hence, the story goes,
he adopted the name of Woodrow Wilson, instead
of Thomas W. Wilson. The former name is
certainly more effective than the latter; but the
interesting phase of the situation is the fact that
according to the established valuation of numbers
in Numerology, no change was made by him in
the Number of Development. The letters of
Thomas W. Wilson produce a total of $55 = 10 =
1$; while the letters of Woodrow Wilson produce
a total of $64 = 10 = 1$.

Having studied Numerological facts relating to
oneself and friends, Numerology should be applied in a practical way that may be helpful to the
affairs of other people; and it may also be utilized
in every-day affairs; but the same constructive
ideals should be constantly kept in mind.

There are many ways in which false application
of Numerology can take place, and these should
be guarded against; for as has been said before,
Numerology indicates and has significance but is
not immutable.

The vibratory numbers of houses, telephones,
trains, ships, suburbs, etc., are all significant to a

minor degree, just as is the vibratory number of the day, month, or year. But no one should be foolish enough to change his place of residence simply because he does not like its vibratory number, nor to wait for a later train, nor to cancel bookings on a steamship. Those are superstitious practices that will react upon the person who employs them, and they must be avoided.

Suppose a race horse has a name which vibrates to the number 5; and that horse is running in the fifth race on the first of March, 1927, which is a day with a vibratory influence of 5, from the number 23. There is no reason why any sane person should bet money on that horse to win the race, because of the peculiar coincidence of numbers.

Numerology is broad and general; not specific. Should that horse win, it could be pointed out as an interesting example of the activity of the number 5; but it could not be cited as conclusive proof that Numerology has predictive powers. On the other hand, should the horse lose, that would not prove that Numerology is fallacious. The principles of an age-old study cannot be treated so frivolously.

The human mind delights to deal in specific examples. That is because people are individuals, not generalities. But any study that treats with humanity as a whole is infinitely greater and broader than the consideration of trivial incidents.

The real object should be to apply the specific to the general, with the hope that the specific example will not be one of the numerous exceptions that occur with every rule. The reverse procedure: namely, the application of the general to the specific will certainly bring great disappointments, even though it may produce correct and harmonious results in a mighty majority of trials.

The possibilities of the system of vertical tabulation, explained in Chapter XX, should not be forgotten in the study of Numerology; for every experimenter may make remarkable and interesting discoveries based upon the application of this peculiar quality of numbers in the affairs of individuals.

XXII. BIRTH NUMBERS OF FAMOUS
PERSONS

The influence of the Birth Number is of great interest to students of Numerology. It is not difficult to reduce a name to its primary number, and thus find the characteristics of famous persons; but considerable research is often necessary to learn the birthdays of notable people.

The Birth Number, which reveals inherent characteristics, is very interesting when studied in connection with historical facts. It frequently shows clearly why certain persons rose to fame, or why they made great mistakes.

Examples are given, herewith, showing the underlying traits of each birth number, and persons who have come under the different vibrations. It is a remarkable fact that virtually every person named showed marked indications of the qualities of his or her particular Birth Number; yet the examples given have been taken at random.

NUMBER 1.

This signifies aggression, and strength of purpose toward a definite goal. It is a great number when inspired by high ideals.

GEORGE WASHINGTON (born February 22, 1732). 2-22-1732. Total 19. Birth Number 1. Washington's determined efforts to succeed in his patriotic efforts are peculiarly significant of the vibratory influence of 1. He was unswerving in his efforts and did not cease until his goal was attained.

NAPOLEON BONAPARTE (born August 15, 1769). 8-15-1769. Total 37, Birth Number 1. Napoleon rose from obscurity and won fame by his powerful, individual efforts. He overcame all obstacles, and his progress is typical of 1; yet his singleness of purpose proved to be his undoing; for he was not content when he had gained established fame.

ENRICO CARUSO (born February 25, 1873). 2-25-1873. Total 28. Birth Number 1. No better example can be given of the power of Number 1. Caruso won unprecedented fame in a single line of effort.

BENEDICT ARNOLD (born January 14, 1741). 1-14-1741. Total 19, Birth Number 1. Here we find the selfish influence of number 1. Arnold was a powerful, dynamic figure. His heroic efforts won the day at Saratoga; but his inherent desire for personal gain led to his dissatisfaction and produced conflicts which finally culminated in his desertion.

NUMBER 2.

This number signifies contrast and peculiar adaptability, as well as balance.

EDGAR ALLAN POE (born January 10, 1809). 1-10-1809. Total 20. Birth Number 2. In Poe, we find all the uncertainty of the vibratory influence of 2. He lived sometimes in luxury; at other times he dwelt in poverty. A man of capability and genius, he never seemed to obtain unity of effort.

ROBERT LOUIS STEVENSON (born November 13, 1850). 11-13-1850. Total 20. Birth Number 2. Here we discover the adaptability, the love of contrast and the ability found in Poe. Yet Stevenson showed traits of balance and equilibrium which are characteristic of 2.

NUMBER 3.

This signifies versatility and expression; a number of natural perfection which carries promise.

QUEEN VICTORIA (born May 24, 1819). 5-24-1819. Total 30. Birth Number 3. In the long life of Queen Victoria, we find continuous examples of the presence of number 3. Her reign was harmonious and brilliant. It did not achieve sudden results or great material gain; yet it was productive of harmony and progress, showing traces of versatility that always seemed to bring about a satisfactory conclusion.

NUMBER 4.

This being a steady, plodding number, is seldom indicative of greatness. Number 3 as a birth number produces versatility; number 4 restricts its possessor to the more commonplace affairs of life.

MARK TWAIN (born November 30, 1835). 11-30-1835. Total 22. Birth Number 4. Mark Twain is noted for his knowledge of human nature, and his outspoken frankness. In all his career he never lost that touch. These are true characteristics of the number 4.

GROVER CLEVELAND (born March 18, 1837). 3-18-1837. Total 31. Birth Number 4. The perseverance of Number 4 is evident in the career of Grover Cleveland, inasmuch as he was the only man to be reelected to the presidency of the United States after missing an intermediate term of office. It is interesting to note that there was a friendship between Mark Twain and Grover Cleveland.

NUMBER 5.

As a Birth Number, 5 brings adventure and unexpected situations. Many famous persons have this Birth Number.

ABRAHAM LINCOLN (born February 12, 1809). 2-12-1809. Total 23. Birth Number 5.

The hazardous times in which Lincoln became president illustrate the influence of 5.

NAPOLEON III (born April 20, 1808). 4-20-1808. Total 23. Birth Number 5. So adventurous was the career of Napoleon III that he has often been referred to as an adventurer. He illustrates the influence of 5 to the fullest degree. In fact, it would be impossible to reconcile his characteristics to any other Birth Number. The coup by which he became emperor; his plans for the conquest of Mexico; and his sudden overthrow may all be attributed to the underlying influence of 5.

BENJAMIN FRANKLIN (born January 17, 1706). 1-17-1706. Total 23. Birth Number 5. The career of Benjamin Franklin was, indeed, an adventurous one; and the times in which he lived were tempestuous. In Franklin, however, we find a modified development of the vibration of 5, in which the qualities of that number were used advantageously.

ROBERT PEARY (born June 6, 1856). 6-6-1856. Total 32. Birth Number 5. Peary's ceaseless thirst for adventure in the exploration of the polar regions clearly shows the influence of 5.

THOMAS JEFFERSON (born April 13, 1743). 4-13-1743. Total 23. Birth Number 5. The influence of the number of adventure is also quite evident in the career of Jefferson.

NUMBER

This is a number of dependability; yet it is a number which holds a restricting influence; and if its bounds are overstepped, disaster often follows. We find it especially evident in the lives of present-day monarchs and executives, and it forms the basis of some interesting comparisons.

THEODORE ROOSEVELT (born October 27, 1859) 10-27-1859. Total 33. Birth Number 6.

WOODROW WILSON (born December 28, 1856). 12-28-1856. Total 33. Birth Number 6.

WARREN HARDING (born November 2, 1865). 11-2-1865. Total 24. Birth Number 6.

These three presidents of the United States were entirely different in characteristics; yet they all possessed the ability to achieve high honor during our present-day period. Each had supporters of high repute, an indication of the vibratory influence of 6; yet that number is found only in underlying characteristics, not in individual actions.

No better proof of this last statement may be found than the comparison of:

KING ALBERT, of Belgium (born April 8, 1875). 4-8-1875. Total 33. Birth Number 6.

KAISER WILHELM II. (born January 27, 1859). 1-27-1859. Total 33. Birth Number 6. These two monarchs both possessed the dependable Birth Number of 6. In King Albert, we find it developed to its highest degree, his actions during and after the great war bringing him higher in the esteem of his people. In the Kaiser, we see the wasting of natural characteristics, and his flight from Germany was a fitting culmination. For many years before the war, the Kaiser was highly esteemed by his subjects.

NUMBER 7.

This mystic number, with its scholarly aspects and difficulty of expression, is not indicative of fame. Two noteworthy examples of its possibilities of attainment are:

JAMES RUSSELL LOWELL (Born February 22, 1819). 2-22-1819. Total 25. Birth Number 7. Lowell was an intellectual man, and the characteristics of 7 are evident in his poetic nature.

HENRY WARD BEECHER (born June 24, 1813). 6-24-1813. Total 25. Birth Number 7. Here was a man who had the ability to develop the intellectual characteristics so typical of 7. He is described as having "susceptibility to culture, love of music and art, a mystical disposition, and an almost feminine tenderness of nature." This description, taken verbatim from a brief biography, is, in itself, a concise summary of the Numerological attributes of number 7. It is an exact indication of characteristics through the application of Numerology.

NUMBER 8.

This is a number of success and material gain. Typical of high constructive ability, it is the Birth Number of many famous persons. Five examples are given herewith; each one is a man who rose to fame and became the most prominent figure in his particular environment.

U. S. GRANT (born April 27, 1822). 4-27-1822. Total 26. Birth Number 8. As commander-in-chief of the Union forces during the Civil War, Grant showed power and ability.

JEFFERSON DAVIS (born June 3, 1808). 6-3-1808. Total 26. Birth Number 8. The fact that Davis was elected president of the Confederacy with very little opposition is, alone, striking proof of the presence of the characteristics of 8.

OLIVER CROMWELL (born April 25, 1599). 4-25-1599. Total 35. Birth Number 8. Cromwell's rise to the head of the Commonwealth in England was a notable achievement. It signified the power of completion found in number 8, for the new order of affairs virtually died with Cromwell.

BRIGHAM YOUNG (born June 1, 1801). 6-1-1801. Total 17. Birth Number 8. The task of organization and development that confronted Brigham Young is hardly paralleled in history. The success which he attained is amazingly characteristic of the power of Number 8.

RUDYARD KIPLING (born December 30, 1865). 12-30-1865. Total 26. Birth Number 8. In Kipling, we find a most remarkable manifestation of the vibratory influence of 8. He had the ability to develop the solid characteristics of that number into prose and poetry, a most remarkable achievement. But just as 8 indicates completeness, frequently followed by a decline, so do we see in Kipling the passing of the prime; a loss of former ability.

Singularly enough, every example given of the Number 8 has this peculiarity. It is a well-known fact that Grant suffered reverses in his later years. Jefferson Davis lost his greatness with the fall of the Confederacy; Oliver Cromwell was facing difficult conditions before his death; and the great power which Brigham Young once wielded was modified and restricted. In all these men, we see a rise to fame followed by the possession of great strength, which finally diminished to a very perceptible degree.

NUMBER 9.

This is a number of high achievement, and universal influence; capable of great possibilities and glory; but also susceptible to dreaminess and impractical ideas.

GUY DE MAUPASSANT (born August 5, 1850). 8-5-1850. Total 27. Birth Number 9. De Maupassant is considered to be one of the masters of modern literature. He had an unequalled ability, a vivid imagination, and a marvelous power of expression, all attributes of 9. Yet his strange career ended in insanity.

JOHN D. ROCKEFELLER (born July 8, 1839). 7-8-1839. Total 36. Birth Number 9. The wealth gained by Rockefeller is somewhat indicative of 8 rather than 9; but his attainments were so unprecedented and so far beyond those of other masters of finance that they can well be attributed to the higher power of 9.

ROBERT E. LEE (born January 19, 1807). 1-19-1807. Total 27. Birth Number 9. In Lee, the finest attributes of Number 9 are in great evidence. He rose to high achievement and powerful purpose; and he commanded high esteem through his work and efforts following the Civil War. The universal influence of 9 is well illustrated in the life of Robert E. Lee.

AARON BURR (born February 6, 1756).
2-6-1756. Total 27. Birth Number 9. Burr was
a man of remarkable ability and influence. He
aspired to great heights and gained prominence in
the face of powerful opposition. The visionary
nature and impractical ideas of 9 are seen in his
career.

CONCLUDING REMARKS

As Numerology, in its modern development, is a comparatively new subject, the person interested in it will find that it will afford many opportunities for experiment and study.

Just a few years ago, the word Numerology meant nothing to the average person. Now it is constantly being quoted in current literature, and every few months shows some new and surprising development.

There is, therefore, a freshness about the subject that makes it extremely interesting. It is unencumbered by vague statements and time-worn fallacies; it has not been foolishly exploited; and it is still open to discussion.

For years we have heard the old question: "What's in a name?" Numerology holds the answer to this riddle, and the application of Numerology has been productive of many remarkable results.

The beauty of Numerology lies in the fact that it can be treated in many ways. People who are mathematically inclined can devote themselves to new calculations. Those who are versed in history may study the Numerology of famous characters. Others may spend their time profitably by checking up the Numerology of their friends and acquaintances; and they may learn important facts if they choose to investigate their own Numerological vibratory influences.

Numerology affords much entertainment. At parties, it is interesting to group the people present according to their Numerology, based either upon the Birth Number, or the Number of Development, or both.

People who have the same Numerology often have much in common. Anyone who studies the vibratory numbers of other people will be impressed by the striking resemblances in characteristics of Numerological doubles. Some may attribute these facts to coincidence. Perhaps they are coincidences. It is a coincidence that both six and five and seven and four equal eleven. Numerology is based upon mathematics, and the science of mathematics abounds in coincidences. There is a mathematical exactness about Numerology, with its chances of error in addition, that is more than significant. Modern Numerology is yet in its infancy. The day may come when the interpretation of numbers will be considered quite as important as simple problems in addition and subtraction.

APPENDIX

Classifications of Numerology

In this section, certain lists of Numerology are given as supplements to the material that has been dealt with in previous portions of the book.

The first is a list of characteristics, followed by the vibratory numbers in which those traits are most frequently found.

Birth Number Table

Activity, 1, 3, 5
Adaptability, 2, 3, 9,
Agreeability, 2, 6, 9
Ambition, 1, 3, 8, 9

Bashfulness, 4, 7
Benevolence, 2, 6

Calmness, 5, 8
Capability, 1, 3, 5, 8, 9
Carelessness, 3, 5, 7
Caution, 2, 4, 6
Changeability, 2, 5, 9
Cheerfulness, 3, 5, 9
Cleverness, 3, 5, 9
Clumsiness, 4

Deceit, 1, 5
Deliberation, 2, 4, 6, 8
Despair, 7
Determination, 1, 8
Dignity, 6, 8, 9

Egotism, 1, 8
Emotion, 2, 9
Endurance, 1, 3, 5
Energy, 1, 3, 5

Analysis, 2, 8, 9
Anxiety, 2, 7
Application, 1, 4, 8
Arrogance, 1, 8

Boldness, 1, 5
Brain-work, 3, 7, 8, 9

Common-sense, 3, 5, 8
Confidence, 1, 3, 5, 8
Conservatism, 2, 4, 6
Courage, 1, 3, 5, 9
Courtesy, 2, 3, 6, 9
Creative ability, 1, 3, 9
Cruelty, 1, 5
Curiosity, 2, 5, 6

Diplomacy, 2, 2, 9
Discontent, 2, 5, 7
Discrimination, 6, 8, 9
Domesticity, 2, 9
Dreaminess, 2, 7, 9

Enterprise, 1, 3, 8
Excitability, 3, 5
Extremeness, 3, 5, 7
Exuberance, 3, 5

Birth Number Table—(Continued)

Fairmindedness, 2, 6
Faithfulness, 2, 4, 6
Fearlessness, 1, 3, 5, 9
Fickleness, 2, 9

Foolishness, 2, 7, 9
Forethought, 8, 9
Frankness, 2, 3, 5
Friendliness, 3, 5, 6, 9

Gallantry, 3, 5, 9
Generosity, 2, 6, 9
Gladness, 3, 5

Gloominess, 2, 7
Good-naturedness, 3, 9
Greed, 5, 8

Harmony, 2, 6, 9
Helpfulness, 2, 6, 7

Honesty, 4, 6, 9
Humor, 1, 3, 5, 9

Idealism, 3, 6, 7, 9
Imaginativeness, 2, 7, 9
Imitativeness, 2, 5
Impartiality, 2, 6
Impatience, 1, 5
Impulsiveness, 1, 3, 5

Inconsistency, 2, 5
Indolence, 2, 7, 9
Industry, 1, 3, 8
Inquisitiveness, 2, 5, 6
Intellectuality, 3, 6, 9
Intuition, 3, 5, 7, 9

Jealousy, 1, 7, 8
Jollity, 3

Jubilance, 3, 9
Justice, 2, 6, 9

Keenness, 1, 3, 5
Kindness, 2. 6, 9

Knowledge, 6, 7, 9

Laziness, 2, 5
Learning, 6, 7, 9

Love, 2, 6, 9
Loyalty, 4, 5, 6

Matureness, 1, 5, 7, 8
Meditation, 7, 9

Memory, 2, 7, 9
Moodiness, 2, 7,

Naturalness, 3, 5, 9

Neatness, 2, 6, 9

Observance, 1, 3, 5
Obstinacy, 4, 8
Originality, 3, 5

Overwork, 1, 7, 8
Overzeal, 3, 5

Patience, 2, 6, 8
Perception, 1, 3, 5
Perseverance, 1, 7, 8

Pride, 1, 5, 8
Procrastination, 2, 7, 9
Progressiveness, 1, 8, 9

Quickness, 1, 3, 5

Quietness, 2, 4, 6

Receptiveness, 2, 6, 9
Recuperation, 1, 3, 5,

Resourcefulness, 3, 5, 8, 9
Restlessness, 2, 5

Self-esteem, 1, 5, 8
Self-reliance, 1, 3, 5, 8
Slowness, 4, 6, 8
Steadfastness, 3, 9

Strength, 1, 8, 9
Stubbornness, 4, 8
Studiousness, 2, 6, 7
Sympathy, 2, 6, 9

Tact, 2, 3, 9
Tenacity, 1, 8
Tolerance, 6, 9

Trustfulness, 4, 6, 9
Truthfulness, 6, 9

Uniformity, 4, 6
Unreasonableness, 4, 5, 8

Unreliability, 2, 5
Unselfishness, 2, 6, 9

Vanity, 1, 8
Variability, 2, 7

Versatility, 3, 5, 9
Vigor, 1, 3, 5

A study of the characteristics of each vibratory number (in Chapters III-XI inclusive) will reveal the particular number in which each of these characteristics is most evident. The preceding list tells the numbers in which the characteristics are quite likely; but certain qualities may be present in other numbers or totally lacking in numbers mentioned. The list gives general indications and probabilities.

The same is true of the second list, following, which names certain occupations, and the numbers best suited to them. The Birth Number is of importance in the first list; the Number of Development takes precedence in the second, but the three notable numbers, Birth, Destiny and Development, should be carefully considered throughout.

Number of Development Table

Accountant, 4, 8
Actor, 1, 3, 5, 7, 9
Actuary, 4, 6
Archaeologist, 5, 7

Architect, 2, 6, 8, 9
Artist, 1, 3, 7, 9
Athlete, 1, 3, 5
Author, 3, 5, 7, 9

Banker, 6, 8
Broker, 1, 3, 9

Business-man, 1, 6, 8

Capitalist, 1, 3, 8
Chemist, 4, 6, 7

Contractor, 4, 6, 8
Custodian, 2, 4, 6

Dentist, 2, 4
Detective, 1, 2, 5, 7

Diplomat, 2, 6, 9

Editor, 3, 6, 9
Engineer, 1, 4, 9
Engraver, 4, 6

Examiner, 2, 3, 8
Executive, 1, 3, 8
Explorer, 1, 5, 9

Number of Development Table—(Continued)

Farmer, 4, 6, 8

Financier, 3, 8, 9

Forester, 1, 2, 4

Geologist, 4, 7, 9

Hotel Manager, 3, 6, 8

Humorist, 1, 3, 5, 9

Illustrator, 3, 7, 9

Inventor, 1, 3, 9

Journalist, 3, 5

Lawyer, 2, 6, 9

Legislator, 2, 6, 9

Manufacturer, 4, 6, 8

Mariner, 1, 5, 9

Merchant, 1, 6, 8

Minister, 2, 3, 6

Musician, 3, 7, 9

Physician, 3, 6, 9

Politician, 1, 2, 3, 8

Professor, 2, 6, 7, 9

Promotor, 1, 3, 5, 9

Railroad man, 3, 4, 6, 8

Realtor, 1, 3, 8

Salesman, 5, 8, 9

Scientist, 3, 4, 6

Secretary, 3, 4, 6

Treasurer, 4, 6, 9

This list of occupations is necessarily limited; but the items that have been named are similar to others that have not been mentioned, so it should not be difficult to classify various other occupations.